# THE PRIMARY CORE NATIONAL CURRICULUM

# The Primary Core National Curriculum

## Policy into Practice

Edited by
*David Coulby and
Stephen Ward*

**CASSELL**

Cassell Educational Limited
Villiers House
41/47 Strand
London WC2N 5JE

First published 1990

**British Library Cataloguing in Publication Data**
The primary core National Curriculum : policy into practice.
   1. Great Britain. Primary schools. Curriculum
   I. Coulby, David   II. Ward, Stephen
   372.190941

ISBN 0–304–31963–5 (hb)
ISBN 0–304–31964–3 (pbk)

Phototypeset by Input Typesetting Ltd, London

Printed and bound in Great Britain by
Biddles Ltd, Guildford and King's Lynn

# Contents

*This book is dedicated to Heather and Jacquie (again!)*

# Notes on Contributors

**David Clemson** taught in primary schools in Wolverhampton where he later became an advisory teacher for primary mathematics. Since 1987 he has been Senior Lecturer in Primary Professional Studies at Bath College of Higher Education and a member of the team teaching mathematics in initial teacher training courses. He is particularly interested in multicultural developments in mathematics.

**David Coulby** is Head of Education Faculty at Bath College of Higher Education. Before going to Bath he had worked at the London Institute of Education and as a teacher in the East End of London. He is interested in educational policy. His most recent book in this area is, with Leslie Bash, *The Education Reform Act: Competition and Control*.

**Richard Fox** has taught on primary language courses for the past five years as Senior Lecturer in Education at Bath College of Higher Education. He has worked as a primary school teacher and as an educational psychologist as well as in teacher education. His research interests are concerned with children's narrative writing and the assessment of the development of children as writers. He is now a Lecturer in Primary Education at the School of Education, University of Exeter.

**Peter Frost** taught in primary schools in Kent before joining Bath College of Higher Education as Senior Lecturer in Primary

Professional Studies. He leads the team teaching the mathematics courses in initial teacher education and co-ordinates programmes for American students and teachers. His interests include classroom teaching and learning and curriculum integration in the primary school.

**Ron Ritchie** worked in industry before teaching in secondary and primary schools. He later became an advisory teacher for primary science in Avon, during which time he was secretary to the Primary Science and Technology Advisory Teachers Group. In 1988 he joined the staff of Bath College of Higher Education as Senior Lecturer in Primary Science and Technology. He is involved in INSET as well as in national projects, including MIST (Modular Investigations in Science and Technology – a Video Disk Project).

**Stephen Ward** taught in primary and secondary schools and a language centre in Leeds before joining Bath College of Higher Education to teach Primary Professional Studies in initial and in-service teacher education. At present he is the co-ordinator of INSET courses at the college. His interests are in teaching and learning in primary classrooms, language in education and multi-cultural/anti-racist education.

**Sally Yates** taught in primary schools in Inner London before becoming an advisory teacher for language. She was involved in the piloting and implementation of the ILEA Primary Language Record and is now Senior Lecturer in Language in Primary Education at Bath College of Higher Education. Her main interests are in working in language with young children.

# Preface

Thanks are due to the many primary teachers who supported us in the production of this book by offering examples of their classroom practice and by sharing with us their ideas about the implementation of the National Curriculum.

We are also grateful to students and colleagues at Bath College of Higher Education who have engaged with us in continuing debate about the many aspects of the 1988 Act.

Special thanks are also due to Chris Hawdon, the computer technician at Bath College of Higher Education, who managed to orchestrate so many discordant word processors.

# *Abbreviations*

| | |
|---|---|
| APU | Assessment of Performance Unit |
| ASE | Association for Science Education |
| AT | attainment target |
| CIP | Classroom Interaction Project |
| CLIS | Children Learning in Science (project) |
| CTC | City Technology College |
| ESG | education support grant |
| INSET | in-service education of teachers |
| IPSE | Initiatives in Primary Science: an Evaluation |
| IT | information technology |
| NCC | National Curriculum Council |
| NSG | non-statutory guidance |
| PC | profile component |
| SAT | standard assessment task |
| SCDC | School Curriculum Development Committee |
| SE | Standard English |
| SEAC | School Examinations and Assessment Council |
| SPACE | Science Processes and Concept Exploration |
| TA | teacher assessment |
| TGAT | Task Group on Assessment and Testing |

# Chapter 1

# The Construction and Implementation of the Primary Core Curriculum

*David Coulby*

## THE NATIONAL CURRICULUM AND THE 1988 EDUCATION ACT

This book sets out to clarify the three core subjects of the National Curriculum – English, mathematics and science – as they will apply in primary schools. In order to do this it explains the debates which took place at the time that the three core subjects were being finalized. It then goes on to consider how the best of primary practice can be preserved within the National Curriculum and indeed how the national framework can provide opportunities for improvement in this best practice. Crucial to this, the book emphasizes the part which primary teachers and heads have themselves to play in the formulation of the National Curriculum. Without this active engagement on the part of the practitioners the national framework will never be successfully filled out.

In approaching the National Curriculum in this way, the book sees it as a major opportunity to be grasped by primary schools. However, unfortunately, the National Curriculum cannot be understood apart from the wider legislation within which it is embedded. Certainly it cannot be separated from the 1988 Education Act, of which it actually forms so small a portion. This was understood by some commentators before the Act was actually passed (see especially Simon, 1988). More recently there has been a tendency to treat the National Curriculum as an isolated topic, as if it existed in a legislative vacuum (for instance, Emerson and Goddard, 1989). Even more worryingly and misleadingly one commentator (Pring, 1989) has attempted to consider the National Curriculum in isolation from its own associated assessment arrangements. The assessment arrangements are actually fundamental to understanding both the National Curriculum and its political purposes.

One of the main purposes of the 1988 Act was to increase differentiation between schools and to encourage competition between them (for a fuller discussion of the issues raised in this section see Bash and Coulby, 1989). Differentiation at secondary level was increased by the foundation of city technology colleges (CTCs) and the establishment of grant-maintained status (the right to 'opt out' of local education authority (LEA) control and receive funding directly from the Department of Education and Science (DES)). For both primary and secondary schools competition was increased through the introduction of open enrolment. This meant that schools could enrol pupils beyond the limits which had previously been established by LEAs. Popular schools could thus increase their rolls and sprout mobile classrooms in their playgrounds. The rolls of less popular schools were commensurately likely to fall and, in some cases, the future viability of schools is likely to come into question. At the same time the introduction of devolved resources and local management of some primary and all secondary schools provided both the mechanisms and the ethos to increase competitiveness between schools.

The encouragement of competitiveness rests on the philosophy that by competing individuals and institutions make themselves strong and effective. It is considered necessary to reward the effective and to penalize the less effective. In the case of primary schools the effective ones will be rewarded with more pupils and resources and the less effective ones will receive fewer pupils and resources and so ultimately close to make way completely for their more successful rivals. The issue at this stage is neither with the moral or economic rightness of this philosophy nor with its appropriateness for application to schools; rather it is with the role of the National Curriculum in the implementation of this wave of educational change.

In this respect it is necessary to consider on what basis the schools will be competing. To a certain extent the terms of the competition will be those of parental gossip and rumour, often enough fed by the tidiness of school uniforms, the success of football teams and the demeanour of pupils on their way to and from school. The National Curriculum will provide much more public and apparently objective terms for the competition than have previously been available. Testing at the ages of 7 and 11 will provide the league tables on which parents will judge primary schools (even though for some schools the 7-year-old results may not be officially published). The National Curriculum is inseparable from its assessment arrangements because these provide the politically necessary criteria on which competition between schools, between teachers and between pupils can be introduced with the appearance of legitimacy. Along with the assessment arrangements the National Curriculum is just one element in a larger political programme.

This book is by no means an unremitting critique of the National Curriculum. On the contrary the authors regard it as an important opportunity for primary schools. However, in examining and developing the opportunities, the wider framework of political change, within which the National Curriculum rests, must not be forgotten.

## THE INTENTIONS OF THE NATIONAL PRIMARY CORE CURRICULUM

The general principles behind the introduction of the National Curriculum as it was originally proposed (DES and Welsh Office, 1987) met with a good deal of political and professional approval. These principles included the advantages of continuity within and between schools and the establishment of a clear curricular entitlement for all children. Opposition to the introduction of the National Curriculum tended to focus on the testing arrangements or on the exclusion of particular subjects from the statutory curriculum. Concern was, however, expressed at the way in which the compulsory curriculum of state schools was to be determined (see, for instance, Simon, 1988; White, 1988). The concern was that the knowledge now to be taught in schools was to be decided finally not by subject experts nor by teachers but by politicians.

The 1988 Act clearly and deliberately gives the power to determine what is taught in both the core and foundation subjects to the Secretaries of State for Education and Science and for Wales. In effect the decisions will be taken by the Secretary of State for Education and Science. It is important to stress that there is nothing intrinsically undemocratic about this. On the contrary, controversial subjects are decided in a democracy by means of the decisions of properly elected representatives. There is little doubt that during the 1970s and 1980s the school curriculum had become an area of political interest and controversy (Coulby, 1989a). It is appropriate then that it should be placed in the hands of elected representatives rather than left with teachers or experts neither of whom have any democratic mandate.

It could be objected that local democratically elected representatives – via local education authorities (LEAs) – might have been better placed to ensure that a common curriculum was also responsive to particular needs and interests of different areas. But this would, even if not to a necessarily damaging extent, impair the attractive notion of a *national* curriculum. However, given that fee-paying schools and CTCs, not to mention Scotland and Northern Ireland, are exempt from the National Curriculum, the case for total Westminster control is considerably weakened. Furthermore, in a general election, it is more than possible that the content of the primary school curriculum might be less influential on people's voting decisions than, say, promises about income tax or defence policy. In a local election educational issues are more likely to have a greater influence on the way in which people vote.

With a school curriculum controlled by Westminster party politicians, there is the risk that there will be major changes in what is meant to be taught in schools each time the government, or indeed the Secretary of State for Education and Science, changes. There is further the risk that the school curriculum will be constructed in a way which is politically partisan. In short, the passing of the 1988 Act made possible the introduction of deliberate political bias into the school curriculum (Coulby, 1989b). There were many who feared at the time that this was actually the intention of the National Curriculum clauses of that

Act (White, 1988). These fears were strengthened by the government's acceptance of the Lords' amendment that compulsory religious education should be of a 'mainly Christian' character, as it seemed like a manifestation of the traditionally Anglican aspect of Toryism. It was anticipated that the National Curriculum which was to be drawn up would be a Conservative curriculum, traditionalist, formal, unintegrated and nationalist.

The Secretaries of State certainly had the power to ensure that this was the case. They were able to appoint the members of the subject working groups as well as the members of the National Curriculum Council (NCC) itself. At the time of the initial NCC appointments the newspapers reported clear political vetoing of appointees, coming, it was rumoured, from the Prime Minister herself. Further, the roles of the NCC and the School Examinations and Assessment Council (SEAC) are anyway only advisory. The Secretaries of State are free to ignore their recommendations, and in some cases did just that. Where this did not happen strict political guidance was given to NCC as to how it should modify the final reports of the working groups. Similarly, firm initial and supplementary guidance was given to all the working groups by the Secretary of State for Education and Science.

After the passing of the Act, then, there was an expectation that the schools were about to have thrust on them a controversial and politicized National Curriculum. This expectation was based on the interpretation of the exclusion of the fee-paying schools and the CTCs from compliance with the National Curriculum; on the precedent of the religious education clauses of the Act which explicitly enforced Christianity as against a multicultural approach to world religions and, above all, on the many and imposing powers which the Secretaries of State had deliberately placed in their own hands. Were these expectations justified by the way in which the core primary curriculum was, in the event, drawn up?

## THE CONSTRUCTION OF THE NATIONAL CORE CURRICULUM

The three core curriculum subjects, mathematics, science and English, were the first to be finalized. The main mechanisms for their establishment were three working groups, one for each subject. It is worth considering these working groups in some detail since they had such influence on the National Curriculum. Before looking at the sequencing of their activities, then, it is helpful to observe their impact on the National Curriculum in terms of membership, structure and time-scale. The working groups were appointed by the then Secretary of State, Kenneth Baker. Their membership had no mandate from the teaching profession, from learned associations of subject specialists or from university departments. They were not in any sense meant to be seen to be representative. However, their membership was widely drawn and did, indeed, include recognized national subject experts, practising teachers (though no primary teachers on the Mathematics Working Group) and representatives of LEAs and teacher-training institutions. There were also members from industry and commerce – that is, from one side of industry and commerce; there were no members chosen for their work in the trade union movement. The membership of the groups, then, was safely if not provocatively right wing but with good representation from specialists and professionals.

The minutes of these working groups have not been made public nor have those of the conversations between the various Chairs and the Secretary of State. These working groups were actually having the definitive conversations about the content of school knowledge in England and Wales and their minutes would make interesting reading for more than those concerned with the politics of the implementation of the 1988 Education Act. A group of people were gathered together to decide what should be the content of major subjects in both primary and secondary schools. Their debates might well have reflected familiar conflicts within each subject area, but the resolution of those debates constituted an unprecedented step towards the finalization of school knowledge. The absurdity of such proceedings should not distract from their significance.

There were surprisingly few leaks from the groups and it would be interesting to know, further, the mode of procedure of the working groups and especially whether they actually split up into sub-groups to determine particular profile components (PCs). If this were the procedure it might explain the resulting proliferation of PCs and Attainment Targets (ATs). Perhaps the chairs of the working groups, beset with demands for the inclusion of material from a range of sub-groups, took the easy route and simply included everything!

But perhaps there is no need to look further than the ridiculously tight time-scales to explain the proliferation of the material. The working groups were composed in the main of people who already had busy jobs; they were attempting to finalize the National Curriculum in a matter of months and doing it in their spare time. In order to prevent proliferation the groups would have had to hone down their early work, looking for overlaps and seeking the most parsimonious formats; they would, further, have had to do this *across* all the groups to avoid overlap and duplication. This work, to judge by the results, was not done. It could not have been done in the time allowed by the Secretaries of State. They, of course, were in a hurry to have some results to show in order to prove their effectiveness to their party and to the electorate.

The major structural decision about the groups, and the one which had most impact on the subsequent shape of the National Curriculum, was one over which the members had little influence. That was the decision to have *subject* groups at all. As Chapter 5 makes clear, a more sensible procedure for primary education might have been to have constructed the national curriculum by phase. The decision to have subject-based groups meant that an unintegrated and secondary-oriented curriculum was predetermined. The subject-base nature of the groups also accounts for some of the proliferation of PCs and ATs. Working in isolation and committed to their own particular subjects, the members were not able to leave out any area of knowledge with the certainty that another group would cover it. The principle became to include everything and, at best, to cross reference it to the recommendations of other groups.

The ways in which the three core areas of the National Curriculum were constructed were subtly and importantly different, although each followed the same broad pattern. The substance of the debates involved in this construction is outlined and discussed for each subject in the three succeeding chapters. At this stage, it is the differences in the process which need to be clarified.

A Mathematics Working Group was established, but its interim report (Mathematics Working Group, 1987) met with the displeasure of the then Secretary of State, Baker. The Chair resigned and the group produced a final report (DES and Welsh Office, 1988a) which went to the NCC with a commentary from the Secretary of State. The NCC carried out a consultation exercise, the results of which it explicitly ignored, preferring to follow the precepts of the Secretary of State. The then Secretary of State Baker consulted rapidly on the NCC advice, published draft orders with no significant changes, again consulted rapidly and produced final orders which once more were not significantly changed.

The Science Working Group's interim report (Science Working Group, 1987) had a more favourable reception from the Secretary of State and they were able to continue under the same Chair to produce their final report (DES and Welsh Office, 1988b). Again stern advice from the Secretaries of State (playing down the ATs for exploration and investigation and for communication and science in action) accompanied the final report on its way to the NCC. Again the NCC explicitly chose to heed this advice rather than the overwhelming results of their consultation – not least in going ahead with two distinct strands for secondary science, one to take about 20 per cent of the timetable but the other only about 12 per cent. More consultation led to draft orders and yet more consultation to final orders with no major change of substance.

The Science Working Group had also been charged with taking a first look at the foundation subject of technology. There are sections on technology in both of their reports. However, once the Working Group on Technology, chaired by Lady Parkes, was established, this subject was more clearly separated from science. The final orders for science are, then, completely separate from those for technology. Thus, in the actual process of construction of the National Curriculum the momentum was towards subject separation and curricular disintegration. The publication of the final report on what, by then, had become design and technology (DES and Welsh Office, 1989a) was one of the points at which the proliferation of at least partly overlapping ATs most clearly emerged. The result of this proliferation was to make the National Curriculum almost unreadable for primary teachers: see the final section of this chapter.

Whilst the Education Bill was still before Parliament a Committee of Inquiry into the Teaching of English Language had been established. The reasons for this were the orchestration of traditionalist fears over changes in the language curriculum which had supposedly resulted in weighty matters such as the neglect of grammar and spelling at both primary and secondary school (see Chapter 2). Given that this committee, chaired by Kingman, was already in operation, it was thought inappropriate to establish a working group. The Kingman Report (DES, 1988) made recommendations which could be interpreted as a reassertion of the importance of grammar in the English curriculum. When a delighted Secretary of State for Education and Science affirmed that the Kingman Report should form the basis for the deliberations of the English Working Group, and announced that the group would be chaired by a member of the Kingman Committee and prominent Black Paperist, Cox, fears about the politicization of the school curriculum were at their highest.

Because of the scramble to have the primary core curriculum up and running in September 1989, the English Working Group published its recommendations for ages 5 to 11 (DES and Welsh Office, 1988c) in advance of completing its work on the secondary phase (DES and Welsh Office, 1989b). There was no interim report; Kingman perhaps being perceived to have done that job. The final reports did not in the event echo the traditionalist concerns of Kingman, advocating instead the adoption of much of the best of current progressive primary practice in the language area, including speaking and listening and the recognition of the importance of non-standard forms of English and of the strengths of bilingual pupils. With the September 1989 deadline for the introduction of the core curriculum to 5-year-olds even nearer, the NCC followed up with ATs and Programmes of Study for the first key stage only (NCC, 1989a). In this case the NCC's changes apparently showed them to be more right wing than the government. It was reported in the press at the time that Cox and his entire group had threatened to resign, leaving their secondary work uncompleted, because of the changes made by the NCC (Nash, 1989). In the event the then Secretary of State, Baker, sided with Cox and the final orders actually saw the reinstatement of the more liberal and professionally acceptable consensus advocated by the working group.

The non-statutory guidance (NSG) issued for each of the three subjects is discussed in the final section of this chapter. In each case the NSG proved to be more progressive than might have been anticipated from the final orders.

The Science and Mathematics Working Groups were the first to be established along with a third more general group, the Task Group on Assessment and Testing (TGAT). The reports of this group (TGAT, 1987; 1988) were influential on all subsequent thinking on the National Curriculum, particularly that taking place immediately after they were published. At the time of their publication the recommendations of TGAT served to reassure many in the profession that national assessment need not be a reversion to crude eleven-plus style testing:

> The assessment process itself should not determine what is to be taught and learned. . . . For the purpose of national assessment we give priority to the following four criteria:
>
> — the assessment results should give direct information about pupils' achievement in relation to objectives: they should be *criterion-referenced;*
> — the results should provide a basis for decisions about pupils' further learning needs; they should be *formative;*
> — the scales or grades should be capable of comparison across classes and schools, if teachers, pupils and parents are to share a common language and common standards: so the assessments should be calibrated or *moderated;*
> — the ways in which criteria are set up and used should relate to expected routes of educational development, giving some continuity to a pupil's assessment at different ages: the assessments should relate to *progression.* (TGAT, 1987, Paras 4 & 5)

The first report emphasized the formative aspects of assessment. A range of assessment approaches, consistent with normal classroom activities and delivered and marked by teachers, were advocated as against short sharp standardized tests.

In a sense the TGAT reports can be seen as an attempt to professionalize the political demand for testing. As indicated in the first section of this chapter the importance of testing in the 1988 Act is far from confined to ensuring the effective implementation of the National Curriculum. The tests were intended as the mechanisms for the introduction of competitiveness into state schooling. The TGAT reports, stressing the positive values of assessment and ignoring the probable negative effects, inevitably came as a relief to other professionals. However, if the relief was any more than short-lived it was the product of wishful thinking. As is made clear later, the line subsequently taken by SEAC (Halsey, 1989) was to replace teacher assessment and teacher-assessed tasks with nationally set tests.

The working groups succeeded in professionalizing much of the National Curriculum, but the TGAT attempt to professionalize testing into formative assessment is doomed to fail. Not only would the costs of the TGAT recommendations be exceedingly high, there would also be a danger that the wider political intentions of the 1988 Act, which stretch beyond the National Curriculum, would be undermined. So the predictions of a politicized National Curriculum were, to an extent, disproved, as subject material was argued among professionals and between professionals and politicians. It is for this reason that this book sees the National Curriculum as an opportunity for primary schools. The testing arrangements, nevertheless, are proving less pervious to professional argument. The National Curriculum must then still be seen as set within a structure of politically determined change which is potentially most damaging to primary schools and their pupils.

However, a good deal of uncertainty still lingers over the whole area of assessment (Coulby, 1989). After the publication of the TGAT reports three consortia were commissioned to draw up the standard assessment tasks (SATs). These consortia were not to report until the spring of 1990. This was particularly unfortunate for those infant teachers who, in September 1989, began teaching the primary core curriculum to 5-year-olds, having some idea of what they were meant to be teaching but no idea how, in two years' time, it was to be assessed.

## SIGNIFICANT DIFFERENCES FROM CURRENT PRIMARY PRACTICE

The National Curriculum could have represented a major improvement in primary schools. However, given the multitude of ATs and the rigid testing arrangements likely to accompany them, together with the whole competitive philosophy behind the publication of results, it seems more likely to be a retrogressive and harmful measure. It is unfortunately not possible to separate the testing initiative from the curriculum initiative. However, it is worth considering initially what difference the National Curriculum will make to primary schools, apart from the assessment and testing. This allows a favourable, but unfortunately incomplete, picture to be drawn.

The first significant difference from current practice is that there should be far more consistency between schools and, in some cases, within schools, than was the case prior to the introduction of the National Curriculum. Teachers entering a primary school for their first year's teaching will be able to have firm and reasonable expectations about what their pupils will have covered. Similarly, parents transferring their child between primary schools, for whatever reason, will be able to have the expectation that the child will fit fairly readily into the new curriculum without leaving any large gaps and without undue repetition.

Further, this consistent curriculum embodies much of what is good current primary practice in some schools. A lot more of it represents the high aspirations of what is possible in primary schools. The extent to which these aspirations are realizable is addressed later in this section. Assuming that they are (a large assumption), then the curriculum in most primary schools is likely to improve following the introduction of the National Curriculum. Whether the delivery of this curriculum results in disappointments will be more to do with the two key issues of integration and assessment addressed later in this section and in other chapters of this book. In terms of wide and deep coverage of a whole range of appropriate and necessary themes, the primary national core curriculum represents, on paper, a potential improvement for a great many schools.

In most schools there will be a dramatic increase in the amount of time that is devoted to scientific activity. As Chapter 4 outlines, the development of science was an important component of emerging positive primary practice. However, progress was undoubtedly slow. In placing science as one of the three compulsory core subjects of the primary curriculum, the National Curriculum has made probably its major positive initiative in the primary phase of schooling.

On the other hand, concern remains over the whole area of assessment. The commitment to systematic testing and the publication of results is the flaw which undermines the National Curriculum edifice. Assessment has always been an important component of successful teaching. The formative assessment stressed by TGAT (see p. 10) allows teachers to know what pupils have learned, what remains to be learned, and how this learning might best be brought about. Without such regular, indeed routine, assessment, teaching could hardly be carried out in an efficient way.

However, this is very different from the systematic, age-specific, national testing now being introduced. Although results at the age of 7 *may* remain confidential to the parents, conversations among them as well as the children will inevitably lead to the open discussion of patterns of academic stratification. Furthermore, the then Secretary of State, Baker, explicitly encouraged primary schools to go ahead with the publication of results at age 7. Those children who are not succeeding with the National Curriculum will be officially recognized at an early age. Few aspects of this recognition will be to their advantage: public labelling may be added to frustration in diminishing their commitment to the official curriculum of the school and in leading them to look for other ways of proving their remarkability (Hargreaves *et al.*, 1975). Public 'failure' at 7 or 11 will all too easily lead to lower aspirations for particular pupils. Children, parents and teachers may reduce their expectations as a result of the official national status given to this premature testing.

The assessment provisions of the National Curriculum are designed to encourage competition between schools, between teachers within schools and implicitly between pupils as well. Not only will there be unfortunate casualties of these competitions but the whole National Curriculum initiative may yet become confused with the ideology of competitiveness. The danger is that what the National Curriculum will teach above all else is competitiveness for its own sake. The rigid assessment stipulations may actually undermine many of the enriching consequences which could flow from a national primary curriculum.

In addition the proliferation of ATs means that a considerable amount of teacher time will have to be spent setting, marking and moderating the SATs as well as completing the increasingly demanding forms and records associated with the assessment of the National Curriculum (DES, 1989). So demanding will this work become that, unless the proliferation of SATs is somehow contained, the time needed to assess the National Curriculum will deleteriously affect the time available to teach it.

It is increasingly becoming evident that the shift to national testing at four ages is a leap in the dark. It is not something that has in any way been previously attempted. The mechanisms being put into place are likely to be highly bureaucratic. It is now clear that where there is a difference between a teacher assessment and the result of a SAT, it is the latter which will be deemed to be correct (Halsey, 1989). The principles of teacher-directed assessment within the normal activities of the school day, apparently embodied in the TGAT reports, seem gradually to be being abandoned. As indicated in the previous section, it is the damaging and politically crucial element of testing which has proved the aspect of the National Curriculum most resistant to professional modification.

A further major difficulty for the National Curriculum in primary schools is that it is perceived and described in terms of subjects. In many ways the National Curriculum framework is that of the previously almost totally discarded grammar school curriculum (Aldrich, 1988). The curriculum is described in terms of subject disciplines which themselves follow an exceedingly traditional pattern of selection. At secondary level subjects such as life skills or economic and political awareness are excluded; for primary schools the opportunities for social studies work are diminished since these do not form an explicit part of the National Curriculum. In the process of attrition from interim reports through to orders most mention of equal opportunities and multicultural education have been lost in the published documents. The loss of a multicultural approach to the curriculum is regrettable since it risks a narrow and one-sided view of knowledge (Coulby, 1985) as well as failing to reflect the diversity of the cities of England and Wales. (However, these issues have re-emerged into prominence in the Non-Statutory Guidance: see the following section.) Although not overtly political, the selection of subjects, and the processes whereby they are being introduced, risk the establishment of a bland, unquestioning, uncritical curriculum at primary as well as secondary level.

The issue of integration is also relevant to both phases but particularly to primary. The very way in which the National Curriculum was drawn up, with separate working groups for each subject discipline, has served to encourage and enshrine unintegrated approaches to knowledge. Although the groups have stressed the need for integration, especially at the primary phase, the lack of communication between them has hardly encouraged this (see Chapter 5). The proliferation of ATs has already been mentioned. The further danger is that there could be actual overlap, as opposed to planned integration, between the various subjects. These may well be ironed out as the National Curriculum evolves. Certainly it is one of the strengths of the National Curriculum that it is not seen to be static but rather the subject of continuous review and refinement. The working groups all acknowledged the need for integration of subjects at the primary phase. Unfortunately the first attempt by the NCC to address this situation, the publication of *A Framework for the Primary Curriculum* (NCC, 1989b) was far from reassuring: see Chapter 5.

The National Curriculum which has been discussed so far is actually something which until September 1989 only existed in documents. Even after that only a few subjects were being taught to relatively few children. The National Curriculum is an ideal which politicians and civil servants hope to put into practice. Although it may not be easy to draw up a National Curriculum which commands any kind of consensus, it is an appreciably easier task than monitoring what happens in classrooms and ensuring that the curriculum is actually delivered day in day out in the primary schools of England and Wales. Will it be possible to implement the National Curriculum?

There are at least three factors which must be considered in attempting to answer this question: firstly, the amount of time in the school day; secondly, the skills that primary teachers have across the National Curriculum; thirdly, the commitment of primary teachers to developing the skills and materials which might allow the National Curriculum to be a success.

Neither the Act itself nor the orders as they relate to primary schools give any indication of how much of the school week should be taken up either by the National Curriculum as a whole or by each component of it. In his speech on the second reading of the Bill in the Commons in December 1987, the then Secretary of State, Baker, did indicate that:

> We do not intend to lay down either on the face of the Bill or in any secondary legislation, the percentage of time to be spent on the different subjects. This will provide an essential flexibility, but it is our belief that it will be difficult, if not impossible, for any school to provide the national curriculum in less than 70 per cent of the time available. The remaining time will allow schools to offer other subject[s] – among them home economics, Latin, business studies, careers education, and a range of other subjects. (quoted in Haviland, 1988, p. 3)

In practice the National Curriculum may actually take rather more than 70 per cent of the school week. Pressurized teachers are unlikely to risk devoting much time to activities which are not stipulated. Again the assessment arrangements provide the key. Teachers and heads know that it is on the basis of the published test results that they and their schools will be judged. In the wake of open enrolment – introduced, simultaneously with the National Curriculum, in the 1988 Act (Bristol Polytechnic Education Study Group, 1989) – pupil recruitment and the very survival of the school may well depend on these results. Given this pressure primary teachers are unlikely to find much time for the teaching of non-National Curriculum material.

The time allotted to each subject has deliberately been kept vague, though it does appear as an element in the guidance given to the working groups. There is little indication with regard to the primary phase that the groups or the NCC have paid much attention to the practicalities of timing. As the ATs proliferate it looks increasingly difficult to see how so much material can practically be fitted into the school year (Moon and Mortimore, 1989). One of the reasons why the orders look like an impressive curriculum may well be that they are aimed in the main rather high: level 4 of AT1 for science, for instance, includes 'formulate testable hypotheses' and 'construct fair tests' (DES, 1989, p. 4). This tendency to aim high is certainly a good fault; indeed the ability of pupils to generate hypotheses and tests should be a central aim of primary education. (See Chapter 5 for some examples of this.) But it could also be that the orders simply represent too much: it remains to be seen whether pupils will be able to reach all the ATs in the time available in school. It would be a pity if the aim of primary pupils developing hypotheses and testing them were to be lost in the uncontrolled proliferation of ATs.

At the time of the introduction of the primary core curriculum it is very much open to doubt whether primary teachers have the skills to teach all the subjects. With regard to science in particular the reservations are profound. A survey carried out in 1989 to ascertain how competent primary teachers felt to teach the National Curriculum found that 'while 81% felt confident about English, 67% about mathematics and 54% about history, only a third were happy with their ability to teach science (33%), music (26%) or design technology [sic] (14%)' (Wragg *et al.*, 1989). Few primary teachers have covered science in great detail in their own education and their actual knowledge of scientific content and methodology is in many cases quite scant.

Whilst there was concern about teacher skills, schools during 1988 and 1989 could hardly complain about lack of information about the National Curriculum. Staffrooms were awash with interim reports and draft orders; specially prepared INSET (in-service education of teachers) material arrived from the Open University; HMI increased their bombardment of paper, apparently worried lest they should be left out of the act; exorbitant numbers of circulars were issued by the DES; LEAs responded with varying degrees of alarm and cynicism, often producing their own material to add to the pile of paper. The result in primary schools was confusion. The mass of documentation without any properly organized INSET meant that primary teachers could not tell where they were meant to be with any core subject. The arrival of the white ring-binders in the summer of 1989 (DES and Welsh Office, 1989c; 1989d; 1989e) along with the NSG certainly improved things but there remains a need for a widespread and in-depth INSET project right across England and Wales if teachers are to be in a position successfully to teach the primary core. This of course would be an exceedingly costly endeavour. Current INSET proposals, based on previously discredited cascade models and with palpably inadequate resources, will in no way meet this task.

The commitment of primary teachers is obviously a related issue. Many may have reservations about the National Curriculum enterprise, particularly as it refers to the testing arrangements for primary children. If they then find themselves being expected to implement this curriculum without adequate training and materials (Wragg *et al.*, 1989), they may well collectively or individually, openly or tacitly, be resistant to the profound changes which are implied. Without properly trained, confident and committed teachers the National Curriculum will remain a documentary exercise.

## POLITICAL INTENTION AND PRIMARY PRACTICE

Behind the National Curriculum clauses of the 1988 Act was an intention to change the knowledge that teachers transmit in primary schools. Was this intention fulfilled in the primary core curriculum which commenced its introduction in September 1989? It is possible that the elaborate if rapid procedures of the working parties and the NCC described in the first part of this chapter did indeed serve to modify the original political intentions. Whilst the Secretaries of State clearly had the loudest voices throughout this process, the inclinations of the profession and of the subject specialists were far from unheard. The core curriculum is recognizably the product of the right in British politics, but, except perhaps for the exclusion of multicultural and equal opportunities aspects, it is not blatantly politicized. There are no signs of a hegemonic, revanchist curriculum, at least not yet. In some cases political intention does seem to have been suborned by bureaucratic process and resisted by professional determination.

This is further evident with the publication of the NSG for all three subjects (discussed in detail in Chapters 2, 3 and 4). While these do not carry the statutory force of the orders, they will sit beside them in teachers' smart white binders and are therefore likely to be highly influential. The NSG comes the closest so far to an integrated approach to the primary core curriculum; it stresses a multicultural approach to the curriculum; it pays attention to equal opportunities issues. The process seems to be that the working groups issue relatively professional and forward-looking interim reports. These are gradually attenuated through political scrutiny and the intervention of the NCC and the Secretary of State. The final orders are then considerably less progressive (though note the anomalous case of English described earlier). But at the next stage of the NSG, prepared by professionals and subject experts, most of the progressive elements reappear intact.

As indicated earlier, the political intentions of the 1988 Act may be further subverted by lack of appropriate teacher skills, by the inertia of the education establishment or even by the individual or collective hostility of teachers. Passing an Act at Westminster and giving teachers a collection of loose-leaf binders does not automatically change what they teach on Monday mornings. Teachers are appropriately regardful of national legislation in that what they teach will change as they develop the appropriate skills and collect current information and materials: but it will change slowly and not necessarily in the predicted or desired direction. Again it is the testing arrangement which may be used to compel teachers to march in step with the National Curriculum. Teachers and schools not complying with the teaching of ATs may become increasingly visible as the tests are applied. However, since these are the aspect of the policy most vociferously criticized by the professionals, it is over these controlling mechanisms that conflict is likely to be most heated.

The National Primary Core Curriculum is in a sense only part-formed. Drawing up the documentation was the easy part of the process. Changing practice in primary schools is a much more daunting job. In this part of the task the influence of the Secretaries of State, the NCC and subject experts will be as nothing beside the individual and collective experience of primary teachers themselves. Their much larger and more difficult part of the task is now being undertaken. This is the point at which primary practitioners will play their crucial role in the creation of the National Curriculum.

## REFERENCES

Aldrich, R. (1988) The national curriculum: An historical perspective. In Lawton, D. and Chitty C. (eds) (1988) *The National Curriculum*. London: Institute of Education.

Bash, L. and Coulby, D. (1989) *The Education Reform Act: Competition and Control*. London: Cassell.

Bristol Polytechnic Education Study Group (1989) Restructuring the education system? In Bash, L. and Coulby, D. (1989), op. cit.

Coulby, D. (1985) Some notes on cultural relativism and curricular planning in a multicultural society. In Slade, I. (ed.) (1985) *Managing Curricula: A Comparative Perspective*. London: London Association of Comparative Education.

Coulby, D. (1989a) From educational partnership to central control. In Bash, L. and Coulby, D. (1989), op. cit.

Coulby, D. (1989b) The national curriculum. In Bash, L. and Coulby, D. (1989), op. cit.

DES (1988) *Report of the Committee of Inquiry into the Teaching of English*. London: HMSO.

DES (1989) *The Education (School Curriculum and Related Information) Regulations 1989* (Circular 14/89). London: DES.

DES and Welsh Office (1987) *The National Curriculum 5–16: A Consultation Document*. London: DES.

DES and Welsh Office (1988a) *Mathematics for Ages 5 to 16*. London: DES and Welsh Office.

DES and Welsh Office (1988b) *Science for Ages 5 to 16.*London: DES and Welsh Office.

DES and Welsh Office (1988c) *English for Ages 5 to 11*. London: DES and Welsh Office.

DES and Welsh Office (1989a) *Design and Technology for Ages 5 to 16*. London: DES and Welsh Office.

DES and Welsh Office (1989b) *English for Ages 5 to 16*. London: DES and Welsh Office.

DES and Welsh Office (1989c) *English in the National Curriculum*. London: HMSO.

DES and Welsh Office (1989d) *Mathematics in the National Curriculum*. London: HMSO.

DES and Welsh Office (1989e) *Science in the National Curriculum*. London: HMSO.

Emerson, C. and Goddard, I. (1989) *All About the National Curriculum*. London: Heinemann.

Halsey, P. (1989) *National Curriculum Assessment and Testing* (letter to Secretary of State Baker, 13 July 1989. London: SEAC.

Hargreaves, D. H. *et al.* (1975) *Deviance in Classrooms*. London: Routledge and Kegan Paul.

Haviland, J. (ed.) (1988) *Take Care Mr Baker! The Advice on Education Reform which the Government Collected but Withheld*. London: Fourth Estate.

Mathematics Working Group (1987) *Interim Report*. London: DES.

Moon, B. and Mortimore, P. (1989) *The National Curriculum: Straitjacket or Safety Net?* London: Education Reform Group.

Nash, I. (1989) Cox 'threatened to resign'. *Times Educational Supplement*, 21 April 1989, Al.

NCC (1989a) *English 5–11*. York: NCC.

NCC (1989b) *Curriculum Guidance 1: A Framework for the Primary Curriculum*. York: NCC.

Pring, R. (1989) *The New Curriculum*. London: Cassell.

Science Working Group (1987) *Interim Report*. London: DES.

Simon, B. (1988) *Bending the rules: The Baker 'Reform' of Education*. London: Lawrence and Wishart.

TGAT Task Group on Assessment and Testing (1987) *A Report*. London: DES.

TGAT Task Group on Assessment and Testing (1988) *Three Supplementary Reports*. London: DES.

White, J. (1988) An unconstitutional National Curriculum. In Lawton, D. and Chitty, C. (eds) (1988) *The National Curriculum*. London: Institute of Education.

Wragg, T. *et al.* (1989) Teachers' worries over national curriculum revealed. *Junior Education* **13** (6) 6–7.

# Chapter 2

# English in the National Curriculum
*Richard Fox*

## INTRODUCTION

The programmes of study and attainment targets for children from 5 to 7 years old (key stage 1) were published in May 1989, to be used in schools from the autumn of 1989. The attainment targets and programmes of study relating to key stage 2 (7–11-year-olds) were to follow in the spring of 1990 and were also anticipated by a report published in June 1989 (*English for Ages 5 to 16*, DES and Welsh Office, 1989). These documents were the outcome of a considerable struggle, both political and academic, which had a long history and reflected very different views of what sort of English children should be learning in primary schools and how they should be taught it. They followed a string of official inquiries and consultation reports on the teaching of English, which can be traced back to the Bullock Report (DES, 1975), and beyond, and which provide the official account of the debate as it surfaced publicly. To understand the ideas which informed the curriculum for English, as it finally emerged, it is necessary to go back to some of the main issues dealt with in these reports.

Throughout the 1970s and 1980s a rift had grown between those who spend their working lives teaching children in the state education system, whom I shall call 'the professionals', and a variety of concerned people on the outside of the system looking in, over the way English is taught. This difference of opinion can crudely be summarized as an argument between progressive and traditional views of English teaching. From the professionals'

point of view it often seemed that the process of forcing through
the programme for a National Curriculum was a politically motiv-
ated attempt to remove their influence from schools and to
replace an enlightened view of developing language competence
with an outdated and misguided version of 'back to basics'. It
would only be fair, however, to try to see things from the other
side of the fence also. There were many outside teaching who
cared passionately about the English language and felt that it
was no longer being taught properly. To such supporters of
traditional language teaching, the move by the Conservative
government to impose a National Curriculum for English seemed
a golden opportunity to 'stop the rot'.

It seems that primary teachers, who are generally very conscious of their responsibilities to young children and their
parents, have always attempted to try to steer a middle road
between the more extreme opinions of the day and, if anything,
have been rather conservative in their practices (Simon, 1985).
Thus, although it is reasonable to say that the professionals
were generally more likely to hold progressive views on English
teaching than the 'concerned outsiders', there were many teachers who doubted the value of change from traditional methods
and concerns, which had, after all, worked well enough for them.
Since most teachers have been relatively successful at their own
specialist subjects they often feel that it would be a betrayal not
to pass on to their own pupils the same sorts of skills and
attitudes which they themselves developed at school. On the
other hand, curriculum innovation often grows out of a dissatis-
faction felt by some teachers and out of their own experiments
in the classroom (cf. Chapter 5).

## THE CENTRAL ISSUES

The central points of dispute, in this debate about language
teaching, may be summarized as follows:

— Firstly, there is a tension between two perfectly reasonable
   aims of English teaching, namely that children should be
   able to use the language fluently and yet also that they
   should use it accurately. The difficulty is that an undue

emphasis on accuracy may stifle fluency, whilst too much concern for fluency might mean that accuracy is forgotten.
— Secondly, there is a conflict between those who want to emphasize the importance of developing the competence to use language, on the one hand, and those who put greater emphasis on the study of language itself, on the other. There is little agreement, unfortunately, on the question of how far, if at all, a knowledge of the structure or rules of language actually helps one to use it in practice.
— Thirdly, there is disagreement on how far teaching should centre, not only on English, but on a particular sort of English, named by its supporters 'Standard English', as opposed to non-standard dialects and also 'heritage' languages other than English.
— Fourthly, there is a difference of emphasis placed on the importance of oral language, as against reading and writing.

At the risk of caricaturing actual points of view, we might say that traditionalists have generally advocated an emphasis on accuracy of use, the study of language itself, the teaching of Standard English, and the importance of reading and writing, rather than talking and listening. Progressives, on the other hand, have in general wanted to encourage fluency, even at an initial cost in terms of accuracy, the actual use of language rather than its study, the acceptance of whatever dialects children bring with them to school, and the importance of talk. They have also shown more concern for the important minority of British children who grow up speaking a language other than English, or who are bilingual on entry to school. Although one could perfectly well hold a traditional point of view of one of these matters and a progressive view of others, or vice versa, there is in fact a tendency for opinions about them to hang together and this is because they reflect different views of language itself.

Language is above all a human affair, diverse, sprawling and open-ended. It depends for its effectiveness entirely on sets of rules, or conventions, which govern the way in which meanings are assigned either to sounds or to written symbols, and yet those rules remain to a large extent hidden, or even unknown to language users, and they are always in a state of change. The work of trying to set out exactly what the rules of a language like English are, and the attempt to collect all the current words in a dictionary, are tasks which bear some resemblance to trying to map the exact coastline of Britain. The general shape of the language and of the coastline are well known and remain pretty much the same over hundreds of years, yet they are also subject to constant, if minor, changes. The coastline is always shifting, with little bits crumbling away here and being added on there. Over the vast periods of geological time it has changed entirely, many times over. Yet maps date fairly slowly, in terms of the human lifespan. No doubt Dr Johnson, compiler of a great English dictionary in the eighteenth century, would still be able to converse with us today, were he present in person, but the sounds and the vocabulary, and even the syntax, of the language have changed vastly since his time. Whereas the language of the King James Bible, the English Hymnal and the Book of Common Prayer were possibly the greatest sources of continuity for generations of English-speakers over the past four or five centuries, any teacher will tell you how remote they are today from a generation of children reared on *The A-Team, Ghostbusters* or *Neighbours*.

Language is much more than just a set of words, for we have (mostly unwritten) rules for combining sounds into words and words into acceptable sentences. Yet even the task of collecting together the words we use in English is one that never quite keeps pace with the rate of change and increase of the words themselves. In 1989 the greatest attempt yet to record and analyse the natural history of English words was completed. This was the publication of the second edition of the *Oxford English Dictionary* (OED), fully computerized. Since the publication of the first edition, in ten volumes, in 1928, some 5,000 new entries have had to be made, yet the editors happily admit that it is still incomplete as a record of the words actually in use today. English has also become a 'world language' and such is the complexity and variety with which it is used that, according to one of the editors of the OED, if one tried to represent all the different versions in use as a set of interesting circles, overlapping where they share common rules and meanings, 'the central intersection would be so small it wouldn't form a language at all' (*Independent* magazine, 18 March 1989, p. 46). In other words, English as a world language exists in many forms and these forms are to a considerable degree independent as they develop along different lines.

Faced with this protean creature of language, which varies across regions, races, social classes and even families, and yet which relies on agreed conventions, the response of some is to call for order and standardization and of others to celebrate the richness of diversity. At the limits of this argument, no one would want uniformity to be carried to such extremes that everyone used exactly the same accent, the same vocabulary and precisely the same grammar. Even to suggest such a proposition is to expose it as quite impossible, and in any case unwanted and absurd. At the other extreme, language quickly loses its fundamental communicative function if the language used by two different people is so different as to be mutually incomprehensible. Thus some common ground is essential. Civilization is to a great extent a matter of imposing human forms of order on ourselves and on nature and there is much to be gained by having some orderliness in language. (The speed and ease with which you can read this text, for example, is dependent in part on the regular spelling with which it is composed.) But humans also resist order and cleave to individuality and even if we were to agree on some version of Standard English, such an agreement would not stop the language from continuing to shift and change over long periods of time and from one region to another. One might as well attempt to legislate that the coastline stay constant.

By and large, the traditionalists in the debate over primary language have supported order and standardization. Hence their clear support for the teaching of Standard English, as a common form of the language, to all children at school. They have tended to see language as ideally fixed and unchanging, having one 'correct' form, from which other versions merely deviate in error. If pressed on this, they would accept that English has developed and changed over time but they might argue that this is at best a process of refinement and enrichment and that much is gained by building on the conventions established by great speakers and writers of the past. Their view of language as a set of words and grammatical rules for generating meaning, which has precedents and traditions and past examples of greatness, leads them to value accuracy in sticking to conventions. To learn to care about correctness in small matters of spelling and punctuation, they might argue, is to begin to learn to care about the greater matters of preserving a language's ability to encode subtle meanings and to express ideas with beauty and clarity. They seem to fear that English is in danger of drifting into a kind of shapeless swamp, in which small differences in meaning are increasingly lost and people lack the ability to put complex ideas into words. Scholarship, commerce, science and law, besides the language arts, all depend in part on an accurate written version of the language and thus it is standards of literacy which chiefly concern such traditionalists. Let a child speak with any accent and dialect but ensure that he or she can read and write in the standard form of written English. This both enables individuals to be responsible, some would say conforming, citizens, and also enables them to take an active part in the great occupations and careers of power and influence in the world. Hence the concern of the traditionalist not only with accuracy but with standard English, and with literacy over and above oracy. The traditionalist's defence of the study of language itself, as opposed to the encouragement of language in use, is not so easy to explain. In a primitive form it consists of the view that one learns a language by learning the vocabulary, the spellings and the grammatical rules off by heart, rather as Latin used to be taught in schools. Then, presumably, the learned rules are supposed to be put to use. This is not how children learn to speak English and increasingly it is not the method used to teach foreign languages, but it is a possible model, which relates to what many people remember of their own schooling. A more sophisticated defence of the function of studying language is that it helps the pupil increasingly to gain a conscious control over the processes of talking, listening, reading and writing which are at first merely intuitive. If one has learnt the rule, and practised it, then one is less liable to make mistakes or to fail to notice mistakes. In the end this question of how far and to what extent the fluent and accurate use of the language is aided by knowing about the structure and rules of the language is an empirical one, that is, it could be tested through research. Such research as has been done in the past has not shown much, if any, advantage for such learning (Wilkinson, 1986) but it is not clear that the research was conclusive or sufficiently searching.

The progressive point of view starts from a less static view of language and one which tends to prefer diversity to uniformity. It tends to dwell on the relativity of language and its changing forms. What has counted as correct usage in English at one time has been seen as incorrect at another. Thus the word 'nice' once meant ignorant or foolish, then came to mean modest, or shy, then fastidiously careful, or precise, and now means pleasant or agreeable. There is no ultimate 'right' or 'wrong' meaning of 'nice' or indeed of any version of English. In the end, English is whatever people say it is, or in other words, the rules are ultimately the rules that are actually in use. This has an agreeably democratic flavour to it: language is made by the people for the people. It is also a point of view which makes it clear that the decision to make one version of English into Standard English is a political one. It empowers those who already use that version at the cost of those who do not. In addition it is clear that it makes little sense to tell children that the way they talk is 'wrong' when it is the way that they communicate effectively with their family and friends and when one realizes that language is a real part of the child's own emerging sense of identity. To the progressive, the child in the primary school needs to build on the language he or she brings to school by developing a wider range of language 'registers' and uses, starting with the oral language which will always be the most frequently used mode. Progressives do not deny that children should learn whatever conventions are counted as 'correct' but that this learning should grow from the base of the child's own language and should not be counted as superior to it.

In terms of teaching English, or language, in the primary school, the battle lines between the holders of what have here been called 'traditional' and 'progressive' views have been drawn across the whole range of talking, listening, reading and writing. The progressives believe that language is not so much a set of skills to be mastered by repetition as a subtle web of rules for making meaning, which are best learned through use. 'Use' implies real use, in which the language should have a genuine purpose and should relate to the child's own developing understanding of the world. Practising skills in isolation, away from the context of real communication, they regard as having the outward appearance of worthiness but actually as being largely worthless. If accuracy is emphasized too strongly at the start of reading and writing, the child is needlessly discouraged from the central activity of generating meaning. Fluency and confidence must come first or there will be no developing output, and without any real output accuracy becomes redundant. What does it gain a child to know how to write if she never in fact writes? What good is reading if the child has failed to learn that reading is a worthwhile activity?

It is the twin subjects of spelling and grammar, however, that have generated most heat in this debate. Spelling is the most visible product of a child's learning that parents see when they visit schools. It is also the dimension of language which seems most dependent on rote learning. How else is one to learn to spell, except by learning lists of spellings and having them tested? The answer to this is, first of all, to consider how many of the words that you can actually spell were in fact learned via spelling lists at school. Of the several thousand words that the average British adult can spell, only a few hundred, at the very most, can have been learnt in this way. It turns out that it is in the acts of reading and writing that we probably learn most of our knowledge of spellings. Once again, the extent to which deliberate learning and practice aids this more natural process is a complex empirical one which we cannot at present answer satisfactorily.

Turning to grammar, the matter is much more obscure. By and large, traditionalists want more grammar and progressives want less. Neither side has paid much attention to what is actually going on in primary schools at present. But in any case, were they talking about the same thing? To the person in the street 'grammar' is a term which seems to be used fairly loosely to refer to spelling, punctuation and knowledge of the names of parts of speech, such as 'noun' or 'preposition'. To the professionals, 'grammar' has a more precise meaning: it means the rules governing word order in a language. More exactly, it includes the rules of 'accidence' which govern the combination of speech sounds into acceptable words and the rules of 'syntax' which govern the combination of words, or parts of words, into sentences. For the most part it is syntax, or word order, which is taken to be the sense of 'grammar' by professionals.

It is clear that we learn to speak our native language without ever learning its rules of grammar. Once again, to those who emphasize the relativity of language, including what counts as correct syntax, and who support the importance of making school activities relevant to the wider world outside school, the study of the rules of syntax seems largely irrelevant to the central task of equipping young children with the competence to use their native languages with wit and fluency. In addition, developments over the past twenty years or so have seemed to render much of the traditional grammar taught in schools out of date, or at least of doubtful value. This has meant in practice that those teaching in schools who knew most about the structure of language have been in considerable doubt as to what it would be right to teach children about it, if anything. No doubt for primary teachers this seemed, in any case, a matter of more concern to secondary teachers. The proponents of 'grammar' appear to believe that it is essential to learn the rules of grammar in order to write well. If they (mistakenly) include the conventions of punctuation and spelling in the term 'grammar' then they have a point, for there is no doubt that children need to learn to spell and to use punctuation. If however they really mean, as they have sometimes said, that they wish children to be taught about sentence structure, then the case looks much more doubtful. All of us talk, and compose sentences in writing, by thinking about the meanings we are striving to express. We do not normally give the rules of syntax a second thought. Indeed the reader is invited to try to construct a sentence, which makes sense of an idea, whilst at the same time attempting to analyse or plan its grammatical structure. It is, at best, an unnatural thing to do. On the other hand, it is true that if we are to discuss or reflect upon writing, or any other mode of language, then we need a technical vocabulary in order to do so. The question then becomes: how much, and how soon, are children aided in their writing by discussion and analysis of examples of writing? Once again the answer is by no means obvious.

## VIEWS OF THE ENGLISH CURRICULUM: FROM BULLOCK TO KINGMAN

In the early 1970s, it is probably fair to say, there was a wide range of opinion about the proper aims and methods of teaching

English and little consensus on priorities. The Bullock Report (DES, 1975), set up by a previous Conservative government worried about educational standards in English, quickly became a landmark in the field. It strongly advocated a view of teaching which rested on the assumption that children become competent users of language primarily through actually using it in real contexts, to communicate meaning. It emphasized that besides reading and writing, which had always been at the centre of the primary school curriculum, language consists of talking and listening, and that it is this mode of oral language which actually makes up the greatest proportion of our real-life use of language. Moreover, children can practise talking and listening, and reading and writing, not only in English lessons, but in almost any and every type of lesson across the curriculum. Language is not only a subject area in its own right but the very medium in which education is carried on. Every teacher, it was pointed out, is a teacher of language. The very term 'English' had become associated with the traditional subject on the school timetable, with the study of English literature in higher education as its highest aspiration, and with practice exercises in textbooks as its everyday reality. The new-look approach, epitomized by the Bullock Report, preferred the broader term 'Language', which had associations with the natural acquisition of language by young children, the study of language in the discipline of linguistics and which emphasized that primary schools, in particular, should be concerned with equipping all children with the intellectual tools of a complete language for life, rather than with the preparation of a few who would one day go on to study Shakespeare and Milton at university.

Bullock was doubtful about the value of exercises in textbooks which merely give practice in using dislocated fragments of language, taken out of any real context, arguing that they 'give the child no useful insight into language' (DES, 1975, p. 171). Instead, the report advocated encouraging children to use language in the real context of classroom activities, such as investigations of the environment or topic work, where the language being practised was really being used to communicate to real audiences for real purposes. Similarly, books should be read because they were worth reading, either as enjoyable literature or in order to learn from them. Writing should be carried out to articulate new ideas and to share and record learning. Talking too, should be encouraged, along with listening, as a basic tool of thought and enquiry, to be used along with the other modes of language right across the curriculum. Drama, in the form of improvisation, seemed to offer great possibilities in stretching the use of both language and imagination and in providing practice in social skills. In short, a rich and living language was to be nurtured by encouraging children to take part in the real business of communication, at their own level and in connection with their own experience. Crucially, the report recognized that teaching was not simply a matter of transmitting knowledge from teacher to (passive) learner, but that, in the realm of ideas at least, 'the learner has to make a journey in thought for himself' (DES, 1975, p. 141).

The influence of the Bullock Report was considerable within the teaching profession. For some ten years it stood as a central guide to practice and training, having largely won over the support of professionals with its carefully thought out rationale and measured judgements. Not all of the recommendations of Bullock were implemented, however, and there was considerable criticism, as well as praise, for contemporary primary practice in a report published in 1984 by Her Majesty's Inspectorate (HMI) named *English from 5 to 16* (DES, 1984). This document formed part of a series called *Curriculum Matters* and it attempted to establish what HMI regarded as 'good practice' in English teaching. Whilst implicitly accepting much of the approach to language teaching recommended by the Bullock Report, HMI criticized the patchiness of the language work going on in primary schools and felt that a clearer, agreed, set of aims and objectives was needed to tackle this. Teachers were also criticized for not stretching the most able children sufficiently and for not providing a diet of sufficient variety in reading and writing. *English from 5 to 16* suggested that one of the aims of English teachers should be to teach pupils about language: 'so that they achieve a working knowledge of its structure and of the variety of ways in which meaning is made, so that they have a vocabulary for discussing it, so that they can use it with greater awareness, and because it is interesting' (DES, 1984, p. 3). HMI invited responses to this document and later published an account of them: *English from 5 to 16 Incorporating Responses* (DES, 1986, 1988). It was plain from these responses that there was far from a clear consensus amongst professionals about the wisdom of attempting to set clear objectives for teaching language or about the value of teaching children about language in the primary years. Most people would agree that children should learn something about language but what, and when, and how much, were questions on which it was hard to find any agreement.

There was considerable professional scepticism when, in 1987 the new Secretary of State for Education, Kenneth Baker, announced the setting up of an Inquiry into the Teaching of English. To many, this sounded like a politically inspired move, rather than a genuine educational inquiry. It was far from clear what such an inquiry would be able to add to what Bullock had already clarified. When it was learned that the committee of inquiry would be chaired by a mathematician, Sir John Kingman, and that its members would consist largely of academics, writers and broadcasters, with the odd industrialist thrown in, it seemed likely to the professionals that this committee had been gathered together to bring about a defeat for progressive ideas in teaching English. A key member was Professor Brian Cox, a professor of English Literature who had co-edited the 'Black Papers' (Cox and Dyson, 1969) denouncing progressive methods of teaching. Professor Cox had written about the importance of maintaining and improving standards of English and he was to play a key role in the shaping of English in the National Curriculum. Of the nineteen listed members of the committee, two were secondary teachers, one was an adviser for English and only one had previously taught in primary schools (DES and Welsh Office, 1988a, p. 75).

In the event the Kingman Report, published in March 1988, was a thoughtful and interesting document, which aimed to shift the balance of the curriculum towards the study of language, and towards the teaching of standard English, without entirely destroying the progress made since Bullock. It attempted to establish a new position in the middle ground of opinion by rejecting any dogmatic return to what it called 'old-fashioned grammar teaching and learning by rote' (DES, 1988a, p. 3). Equally, it put up a strong case for the importance of children learning about the rules and conventions governing language, dismissing the views of extreme relativists, or those who believed that 'any notion of correct or incorrect language is an affront to personal liberty' (1988a, p. 3). Probably the activity which most traditionalists had hoped to see supported by Kingman was 'parsing', or 'grammatical analysis', in which sentences are taken apart and the parts labelled as different species of clause and phrase. The clauses and phrases can then be further analysed in terms of their parts of speech. In place of this, Kingman in effect suggested that children should learn something of modern structural linguistics. The report produced the outline, or skeleton, of a 'model of language; which described the main elements of the language, together with the way in which the process of communication takes place, how language is acquired and the nature of historical and regional variation.

Kingman also compromised in recommending clearly that the study of language should not become an arid series of exercises, practised out of any real communicative context. Instead it was recommended that language should be analysed and discussed in the context of reading texts and writing for a purpose. The report accepted that the primary objective should be to teach children mastery of language in use but added that even if mastery could be achieved without a study of the structure of language, nevertheless 'there is no positive advantage in such ignorance' (p. 4). The report went on to add:

> And since we believe that knowledge about language, made explicit at that moment when the pupil is ready, can underpin and promote mastery as well, the argument [for teaching children about language] is even stronger. (p. 4)

In this way, without citing any research evidence, but relying on their own convictions, the members of the committee defended the view that learning about language is a necessary and worthwhile part of the primary language curriculum. The question then becomes: what should children be learning about language and at what ages?

The second chapter of Kingman expresses with considerable style the basic reasons for the importance of language in the lives of human beings. It also defends the value of learning about how language works, as a subject of intrinsic interest, particularly when that learning grows out of children's own curiosity and play with language and takes the form of 'an exploration of the language pupils use' (1988a, p. 13). If we encourage children to observe and learn about their environment, or about the structure of the atom, why not also teach them to observe their own language and to take an interest in its structure? The report then goes on to defend the importance of standard English and attempts an interesting definition. The committee had written of the necessity for a standard language as adults move from their localized speech communities into a wider world and now argued that:

> This must be the language which we hold in common, which we call Standard English. All of us can have only partial access to Standard English; the language itself exists like a great social bank on which we all draw and to which we all contribute . . . When children go to school for the first time, their language may differ in many respects from Standard English, depending on where they live, their parents' speech habits, and so on. This is natural and proper and a source of richness. However, one of the schools' duties is to enable children to acquire Standard English, which is their right. This is not a matter of controversy: no item of evidence received by the committee contained disagreement with this point. (1988a, p. 14).

Most importantly, the committee continued by identifying Standard English with the written form of the language. It made clear that we must not confuse Standard English with a 'posh' accent, as it is sometimes called, but instead concentrate on the standard written form of English which is used to communicate all over the world. This defence of Standard English (SE) deserves further scrutiny. By identifying SE with the written form of the language, Kingman takes much of the heat out of the debate about the legitimacy of different spoken dialects. The report also presents the case for teaching SE to children in a positive way: it is 'enabling', and to learn it 'is their right'. One might complain that the quotation above starts by talking about 'localized speech communities' and the general use of the language in the adult world and then slips into treating SE only as a written form, a lesser claim, which would not satisfy many traditionalists. Nor is it clear that the written forms of English used all over the world in fact do share all of their conventions. American spellings, after all, are often distinctive, and even syntax has many local variations. As to the claim that no one dissented from the notion that children should be taught SE, no doubt it all depends upon how the question is put. 'Do you agree that it is desirable for all children to emerge from school able to use the commonly agreed conventions of written English?' is a question unlikely to attract the answer 'No'. But if one were to ask: 'Do you agree that children should be taught the structure of sentences and terminology of linguistics from the beginning of their primary education?' then another range of answers could confidently be expected. Kingman makes a brave attempt to present the 'acceptable' face of SE and promotes, in general, a sensible approach to its place in school. Its treatment of the subject is unlikely to appease any of those who hold more extreme views, however, and it does not really resolve the difficulties of how it should be taught.

Much of the Kingman Report remains, at the present time, an interesting but largely untested set of ideas for strengthening the teaching of English, which have been pushed, at least temporarily, into the background. Kingman attempted to show, in Chapter 4, how the model should be put into use in the classroom and this is where the report is perhaps at its weakest. No doubt the lack of primary teaching experience among the committee's members explains the slightly musty and unconvincing flavour that some of the examples possess. Some uncontroversial examples of early writing by a 7- and a 6-year-old are placed alongside an underdeveloped, limping piece by a 15-year-old boy, the deficiencies of which are then used to demonstrate what linguistic knowledge might be relevant to such a pupil and to his teacher. The teacher, the committee suggests, must decide what to comment on, and which technical terms might be useful to this author at this moment in time, but it shrinks from providing any clear idea of the amount of such teaching or its exact form or when, in the whole age range from 5 to 16, it should occur. A central weakness at this point is the report's lack of a clear view of teaching method, or 'pedagogy'. It has been common for those outside teaching to argue for the inclusion of some or other item of content in the curriculum but then to step back and suggest that it is 'up to teachers' to decide how that content should be taught. But it is not so easy to disentangle content from method (see Chapter 5).

It may be thought unfair to criticize the Kingman Report in this fashion, for after all it was charged with considering English teaching right across the age range from 5 to 16, and it was not the job of the committee to produce a working manual for teachers. However, since the interest in the discussion about teaching children about language centres very largely, as argued above, on detailed questions to do with How much? When? and How?, the Kingman Report's failure to deliver a satisfactory answer to these questions, as they apply to the primary school, makes it less convincing than it otherwise might have been. The report describes with evident approval a lesson for some 7-year-olds, mostly of Asian origin, in which the children discuss suitable words to use as captions to some pictures which describe the story they have been read. They discuss both English and Urdu words and go on to make a list of some words with opposite meanings. No doubt many teachers reading this will have asked themselves: Is this really what all the fuss is about? Is this what is meant, at the end of the day, by 'knowledge about language'? If so, then most primary teachers are already attending to it. But it was not all, and the Kingman Report goes on to list, in Chapter 5, a series of Attainment Targets for children at the ages of 7, 11 and 16 which go much further in specifying what the committee meant by command of language in use and knowledge about language.

Kingman specified twenty-eight targets for 11-year-olds, thirteen about knowledge of language and fifteen about language performance. For 7-year-olds there were twenty-one targets, ten concerning knowledge of language and eleven concerning language performance, or language in use. The exact number is unimportant but the variety of the targets and the range of competence and explicit knowledge which they cover is considerable and may well have seemed impractical to those considering the introduction of a national and nationally tested curriculum. The committee hoped that assessment, wherever possible, should be embedded in the normal work of the classroom. Positive achievements should be stressed and a wide variety of language tasks and situations sampled. It is in such passages as these (DES and Welsh Office, 1988a, pp. 56–9) that all the unresolved problems and contradictions of national assessment are to be seen. It is difficult to see how such a large body of knowledge could be adequately tested in primary classrooms without making major inroads on time and energy.

## PROPOSALS FOR A NATIONAL CURRICULUM

The English Working group set up to make concrete proposals on the content and assessment of English in the National Curriculum was chaired by Professor Cox, mentioned earlier in connection with the Kingman Report, and its recommendations have thus come to be referred to generally as 'the Cox Report'. This document, *English for Ages 5 to 11* (DES and Welsh Office, 1988b) was published in November 1988 and proved to be a far more liberal account than many professionals had feared. The notion of Standard English which had been worked out in Kingman became, in a modified form, the linchpin of the proposals. The working group endorsed Kingman's view that: '. . . it is a clear responsibility of the English curriculum to extend children's use of varieties of language, to develop their capacity to understand written and spoken Standard English and to teach them to write in conventional Standard English' (DES and Welsh Office 1988b, p. iii). It added that:

> The objectives should be to ensure that, by the end of their period of compulsory education, pupils can appreciate the differences between the forms of spoken and written English and their appropriate use, and in particular that they are equipped for adult life and employment by being able to write formal Standard English. (1988b p. iii)

It will be noticed that here Standard English is 'spoken' as well as 'written' and this will be commented on further later.

To the amazement of many professionals it seemed that prolonged contact with those actually teaching and writing about primary-aged children had transformed the government's advisers into enthusiasts for the kind of language work recommended by the Bullock Report. The Cox Report even begins its chapter on 'English in the Primary School' by quoting the famous maxim from the Plowden Report (1967), the very motto of the progressive child-centred primary tradition: 'At the heart of the educational process lies the child.' The lion, it seemed, was lying down with the lamb and even borrowing its ideas. The key assumptions of the Bullock tradition were all endorsed, one after another, by Cox. Oral language was given a prominent place and judged to be as important as literacy. Teachers should build on the successful features of pre-school language acquisition in the home. Development in the four language modes was accepted to be complex and non-linear (the point of this being that it calls into question any attempt to describe that development in terms of a simple list of age-related attainments). English should not be seen as an isolated subject but its aims pursued in activities stretching right across the curriculum. The different language modes should not be practised one by one but 'integrated in good classroom practice'.

Finally, assessment should enable pupils: 'to show what they can do in realistic activities that themselves contribute to learning'. The working group had tried to avoid assessment targets 'which might have undesirable effects in the classroom, for example the use of decontextualized language exercises or other activities of an arid kind' (p. 2).

In comparison with Kingman, much less was said in Cox about knowledge about language, as opposed to language in use. Allen (1988) was quoted repeatedly and at length, one of his claims being that: 'The main job of the teacher responsible for the growth and development of pupils' language is to enable the child to speak, listen, read and write effectively' (p. 6).

Nevertheless, in its third chapter, the Cox Report set out broadly the same case as Kingman for children to be able to analyse and talk about language as well as merely use it. This would be essential if children are to grow up as critical thinkers in a democracy, able to appreciate the ways in which language can be used persuasively, for example. But the spirit of the Cox Report is well captured by its approving quotation from Sybil Marshall (1970), a respected 'progressive' primary teacher in the 1960s: 'I wanted to build up in children a love of English, not merely a knowledge of it.'

Teaching children 'linguistic terminology' is given a chapter to itself in Cox and here it is emphasized that such terminology should be taught in the context of real communicative activities, rather than as an end in itself. What is required is 'systematic discussion of language in use' (DES and Welsh Office, 1988b, p. 21). This provides children with the technical terms they need to become consciously aware, as opposed to only intuitively aware of the way their language works. Verbal labels help us to organize our thinking and help us to reflect in a detached and objective way on the language we normally use automatically.

The study of the different languages and dialects brought by children to school also encourages tolerance of linguistic diversity and a respect for different languages, all of which are rule-governed and systematic. Linguistic terms are also useful for discussing children's writing and 'it is very plausible that children's writing will be improved if they know more about language in general . . .' (1988b, p. 21).

Clearly Cox wanted to encourage a far broader investigation of language structure than the labelling of parts of speech. The authors comment on the way in which, so often, there is a tendency for people to reduce 'knowledge about language', firstly to 'grammar' and then to isolated 'parts of speech'. The authors mention many examples of linguistic terminology but resist the temptation to make a discrete list of those they want taught in primary schools.

Cox showed considerable sensitivity to language diversity and multicultural issues, endorsing Bullock's message that: 'No child should be expected to cast off the language and culture of the home as he crosses the school threshold' (DES, 1975, p. 286).

All pupils should discuss the multicultural nature of British society, and the presence of many children who are bilingual and/or biliterate should be seen not as a problem but as 'an enormous resource'. Nevertheless, all children need to develop gradually from the local varieties of language used in their family and local community to command of those varieties used nationally and internationally. The basic justification for teaching Standard English, according to Cox, is that it enables pupils to do more. 'They can do more when they have a mastery of Standard English because they can communicate in a wider circle both socially and geographically' (DES and Welsh Office, 1988b, p. 11). On the other hand, Cox admitted that too great an emphasis on SE too early on in a child's education could sow the seeds of alienation from school.

Following Kingman, the authors firmly asserted that all children should learn to write in SE, and to be able to understand it, but they drew back from the brink of demanding spoken SE as part of everyday classroom life. Spoken language is largely intuitive and automatic, in terms of accent and dialect, and it would be unrealistic to expect young children suddenly to be able to control consciously these features of their speech.

Instead, teachers should help children to 'move towards spoken Standard English on occasions when they will need to use it . . .' (1988b, p. 14) and it is assumed (a large assumption) that children will want to do this in order to join social groups which they respect. Thus, in Cox, the concept of SE is widened to include a particular dialect of spoken, as well as written, English and this is to be encouraged by the English curriculum on the grounds of giving pupils greater freedom to communicate. The spoken variety should be understood by all, but its use in speech is only to be gradually encouraged, in appropriate contexts. Even in the case of writing, great sensitivity is needed by teachers, who should not treat dialect usages as 'errors', and who should always be alert to the impact of evaluative judgements on the pupil's personal and social identity.

A curious but enlightening feature of Cox is its treatment of Welsh, or rather English in the primary schools of Wales, which is given a chapter to itself. Throughout the official documents on English in the National Curriculum, Welsh is given a special status. Welsh is commonly taught as a first language and is used as the language of instruction in many Welsh schools and yet children manage to cope with English as a second language so successfully that their attainments in English at the age of 11 are broadly on a par with those of other British children. English is generally introduced as a subject and medium at about the age of 7 and so the attainment targets at age 7 for Welsh-speaking children are made a special exception. The acceptance, and encouragement, of this teaching in Welsh makes it necessary to make special conditions and rules for such schools throughout the legal documentation on the National Curriculum. But if Welsh, why not many of the other languages spoken by British children as their 'mother tongues'? Why not Urdu, or Punjabi or Cantonese, or Italian or Gaelic? It seems entirely logical that if all languages are 'equal' in status, and if language diversity is to be seen as an 'enormous resource', then all the languages used as community languages in Britain should be officially supported and encouraged. However, it is not to be. It seems that here political pragmatism takes over and some languages, notably Welsh, are 'more equal than others'.

Speaking and listening are accepted by Cox to be of central importance to intellectual growth and language competence.

Good standards of oracy are demanded by employers, as well as being recommended by teachers. Oracy is given greater prominence in GCSE exams than in the older O-levels and CSEs. The great difficulty with oracy, however, is that its assessment is particularly difficult. Speech, and comprehension of speech, is very much a function of situation and context. The ephemeral nature of talk makes it harder to 'capture' than writing, and tape-recording in classrooms, though feasible, is somewhat difficult and cumbersome. It is also difficult to set out clear and simple targets for increasing levels of oral competence beyond the elementary stages. Here, as in so many places, the high aspirations of the working group come up against the government's insistence on assessment targets and testing. Cox held out for quite complex and varied assessment tasks for speech, relating it to different functions, such as description, instruction, explanation and evaluation, and to different audiences and settings. The group also wanted oracy to be given equal status with literacy at both 7 and 11, an aim they achieved in spite of initial opposition from the Secretary of State.

The treatment of reading, in Cox, shows a tremendous shift from the attitudes of Kingman, in which the teaching of reading was not given much emphasis at all and the study of 'literature' was emphasized. In Cox it is clear that the contemporary view of the professionals, that reading is an active, complex process of using language and thinking to obtain meaning from print, has been accepted. Little is heard of the more traditional 'skills' approach, based on the gradual mastery of 'phonic rules'. Instead the process of reading is described in Allen's (1988) terms, as follows: 'active, creating, hypothesising, weighing the evidence, an individual construction, influenced by the meanings available in the culture'. Schools are encouraged to create a 'dynamic reading environment' and to encourage positive attitudes to reading, that is to say, a love of books. Faced with the near impossibility of stating exactly what children should be able to read at different ages, the working group resorts to broad statements such as that children should: 'read regularly over a wide range of prose and verse' (DES, 1988b, p. 42). In the attainment targets, general reading is differentiated from 'reading for information', a distinction which was to be removed at the following stage of the National Curriculum's construction. The assessment of reading ability was again treated according to the current policies of the professionals in the field, traditional reading tests being criticized and miscue analysis endorsed. In terms of record-keeping, Cox recommended that a common national scheme was needed and suggested that the recently published ILEA *Primary Language Record* (1988) be adopted as a starting point.

In the chapter on writing, especially, it is clear that whoever actually wrote the working group's report had largely been converted to the professionals' point of view. One of the most dynamic and interesting developments in English teaching in the late 1980s had been the new approach to teaching writing embodied in the National Writing Project (a progressive, developmental approach to children's writing) yet this received barely a mention in Kingman. In Cox its ideas are dominant. The aim of fluency is accepted as prior to that of accuracy. In the words of Cox: 'Children cannot be expected to learn everything at once. A measure of tolerance of errors in different language tasks is essential' (DES, 1988b, p. 46).

Moreover the 'secretarial aspects of writing', notably spelling, handwriting and punctuation, 'should not be allowed to predominate in the assessment while the more complex aspects of composition are ignored' (1988b, p. 46). This is the very same argument used in Bullock, which advisers and teacher trainers had been trying to press on teachers and students for the previous fifteen years.

Teachers should at first accept invented spellings and should respond first and foremost to the content, or message, contained in a child's writing. Children need to be given a wide variety of writing tasks, for different audiences and different purposes. Children should be encouraged to behave like real writers, and teachers should write alongside them. Redrafting and editing, the sharing of work between pupils, and classroom publishing should all be encouraged, as should the provision of a proper environment for writing in the classroom. All of the examples of writing variety and development used in Cox were taken from the National Writing Project and illustrate, amongst other things, the use of 'emergent writing' instead of copying and tracing, as the starting point for teaching writing. In dealing with what children should write about, Cox once again echoes the spirit of Bullock in saying that there should be: 'a range of subjects that spring from their own interests and experiences and from the unfolding activities of the classroom' (1988b, p. 52).

There are further sections in Cox on literature (in which a number of authors are 'approved' as good examples) on bilingual children, children with special educational needs, drama, media studies and information technology. Briefly, Cox argued for support to be given to children whose first language is not English, in the form of bilingual teachers in the classroom, amongst other things. The same attainment targets in English, however, were firmly supported as appropriate to all children (except the Welsh at the age of 7, who are exempted from all aspects of English at key stage 1). The use of English is seen as crucial to the success of equal opportunities. For children with special needs, Cox accepted that some of the attainment targets should be waived, although children should be encouraged wherever possible to achieve whatever they can. The means by which the large number of low-attaining children might be helped to reach the standards presently achieved by children of average attainment, however, is scarcely addressed. Drama, media studies and information technology are all accepted as valuable parts of the English curriculum, but it is fair to say that they are not given a major role in the National Curriculum, as set out in Cox. Indeed Cox is at pains, throughout, to emphasize that there is much more of value to be taught in English than can be encapsulated within the bounds of a nationally prescribed curriculum.

The rationale for English in the National Curriculum and the Programmes of Study set out in Cox may be criticized in detail, but their broad outlines were fully in line with the best contemporary practice and were generally endorsed by the professionals. At last, it seemed, those in authority had paid some attention to what the professionals thought really mattered in primary language work. There were three important qualifications to this rapture, however. Firstly, the programmes of study came up against a partly immovable obstacle, in the shape of the attainment targets and the testing of those targets which Cox was obliged to include. Secondly, the reaction of the popular press to Cox showed the huge gap which exists between the professionals and those whose children they teach, by characterizing Cox as a return to all the supposed faults of the 'progressive' teaching of the 1960s. Thirdly, the Secretary of State was clearly worried by the line that Cox had proposed and immediately insisted on a number of modifications, each of which was designed to reinforce 'traditional' concerns. The National Curriculum Council was in an ambiguous position here, being instructed to modify various aspects of the Cox Report by the Secretary of State and yet supposedly representing the point of view of professionals.

The Secretary of State's Foreword to The Cox Report made it clear that he, and no doubt his advisers, had some reservations about its proposals and intended to change them. Firstly the Secretary of State wanted clearer and more specific statements of attainment to be devised, no doubt in order to make them easier to assess. Secondly, more examples were needed to make clearer the differences between levels of attainment proposed. Thirdly, the first target for writing was to be 'strengthened to give greater emphasis to pupils' mastery of the grammatical structure of the English language'. Fourthly, a higher weighting should be given to reading and to writing at the age of 11 than to talking and listening. The programme of study for reading needed to be made more comprehensive and that for writing needed a greater emphasis on grammar and linguistic terminology. Thus, in a series of swift blows, the balance was to be swung back towards the traditionalist concerns of accuracy, literacy, grammar and the testing of attainment.

John Rae reacted to the publication of Cox in an article in the London *Evening Standard* of 17 November 1988, in which he began: 'After 20 years of permissive education of telling children there is no such thing as right and wrong, along comes a report on the teaching of English in primary schools that perpetuates this most damaging fallacy of the Sixties.' His article accused the working party's report of being written by those 'with a vested interest in not condemning the sloppy teaching of English in our schools'. He argued that children should simply be taught what is right, in language, and what is wrong. The unfortunate Professor Cox was interviewed in *The Sunday Times* (20 November 1988) and was clearly partly confused and partly outraged to have been turned by the media in one day from an 'old-fashioned blimp' into a ' woolly liberal'. One of his most revealing comments in the interview was the following: 'Very few people unconnected with primary school have any idea what teachers of five to elevens now face.' It would appear that his own closer acquaintance with the practices of classroom life had enabled him to produce a humane and sensitive report, in which a reasonable compromise was sought between the progressive and traditionalist points of view. But it also seems that this was too great a shock for the popular press, which is written mostly by journalists who were successful under the traditional system. And no doubt they know their readers.

## DRAFT AND FINAL ORDERS FOR KEY STAGE 1

Following a consultation exercise the National Curriculum Council produced a consultation report, *English 5 – 11* (NCC, 1989a). It recommended merging the two attainment targets for reading suggested by Cox into one and made a number of detailed changes to the statements of attainment and programmes of study. Press reports suggested that this NCC consultation report became the subject of a furious row between the Chairman of the NCC, Mr Duncan Graham, and Professor Cox, who thought that his report had been subtly changed to produce a cruder, more didactic approach. According to the same report, Professor Cox succeeded in persuading the Secretary of State, Mr Baker, to restore much of the emphasis of his own original report when it came to making the actual draft orders for legislation to Parliament. Although this hardly seemed to be borne out by the wording of the orders themselves, such details are unimportant beside the fact that such an argument should occur. As the *Times Educational Supplement* remarked: 'That Mr Baker bowed to Professor Cox, the former Black paper author, in defending a broadly liberal consensus in the teaching of English will undoubtedly be seen as the supreme irony' (21 April 1989).

The draft order for key stage 1 for English was published in March 1989 and the final order, after a very brief period of consultation, in May. This was the last opportunity, in the initial cycle of producing a curriculum, for the Secretary of State or his advisers in the NCC or the DES to make significant alterations to the English curriculum for children up to the age of 7. In the event, fewer changes were made than had been forecast. Press speculation had suggested that Mr Baker was determined to reshape the proposals in a more traditionalist form but, following a long discussion at the NCC, it seems that he was persuaded to accept the bulk of the NCC document.

The five attainment targets were retained, relating to speaking and listening, reading, writing, spelling and handwriting. The associated programmes of study were condensed and brief, listing the overall rationale, the materials and the activities which should be covered. An old joke suggests that the definition of the dromedary should be: 'a horse designed by a committee'. Certainly the language of the draft orders is lumpy, unfriendly and too brief to provide much support for teachers seeking guidance. The issues of bilingualism and gender are barely mentioned and drama is pushed to the margins. There is none of the style of Kingman or Cox and, presumably because these orders relate only to the key stage 1, standard English is not even mentioned.

The final orders differ from the draft orders only in matters of detail but the style of writing is certainly more fluent and some of the details are significant. Thus, for example, for attainment target 1 (speaking and listening) at level 2, pupils in the draft orders are required to: 'respond to a wider range of more complex instructions'. In the final orders this is changed to: 'respond appropriately to a range of more complex instructions given by a teacher, and give simple instructions'. The examples accompanying the attainment targets and programmes of study in the final orders are also set out more clearly. Moreover the general spirit behind the Cox Report is preserved, in that speech and listening are given equal weighting with reading and writing, speech is to include talking for learning as well as the 'performance' of set pieces and talking in collaborative group work is encouraged. Furthermore reading is to be developed from oral competence and is to include worthwhile books, poetry, print from the environment and the writing of other pupils. Reading is discussed in terms of the quality of the reading materials, the need to use a range of cues to get at meaning, the importance of discussion about meaning and the evaluation of texts. The importance of links between home and school in teaching reading is noted. It is emphasized that writing should include emergent writing and that teachers should write alongside children. A tremendous variety of types of writing is recommended, as is the discussion and sharing of writing and the publishing of books and other types of writing. Redrafting is to be encouraged and there is support for writing in other curriculum areas, such as science.

There are also some traditional notes sounded here and there in the draft and final orders. There is a repeated demand that speech should be audible and the assessment of speech includes assessment of pupils' ability to respond appropriately to instructions of increasing complexity. Knowledge of the alphabet should be demonstrated at level 2 and punctuation should be given proper attention. There are occasional signs of the struggle to include at least some elements of 'the mastery of grammar'. Thus the statements of attainment for writing suddenly veer from general propositions to the level of the highly specific: at level 3 pupils should learn to connect sentences together with a wider range of words than simply 'and' and 'then'. Similarly at level 3, the revising and redrafting of writing should pay attention to the consistent use of tenses and pronouns.

In the programmes of study it is made clear that pupils should recite poems that have been learned by heart and 'should be taught grammatical terms like sentence, verb, tense, noun, pronoun'. These vestiges of the traditionalists' case, however, are to be found embedded in a proposed curriculum which is very close to the sorts of recommendation made in the Bullock Report. In many ways this appears to represent a victory for the more progressive 'professional' point of view, though the curriculum can also be described as moderate and 'mainstream' in its general outlook. In June 1989, the second report by the English working group, chaired by Professor Cox, was published. This made recommendations for the secondary, as well as the primary, English curriculum, taking matters up to the age of 16. It followed closely the style and policies of the first report and went over some of the primary ground again. On this occasion the Secretary of State endorsed the report without reservation, though he showed his sensitivity to possible attack from the traditionalists in commenting that: 'Grammar and Standard English have a key place'.

The NCC also published non-statutory guidance on teaching English for key stage 1 in June 1989 (NCC, 1989b), which aims to show teachers how to go about planning and implementing the curriculum. At first sight these guidelines seen rather forbidding as, once again, they list all the multifarious demands being made on teachers' time and energy. Rather than providing guidance they seem to constitute a catalogue of requirements. They are full of advice such as follows: 'Children also need to develop, through experience, guidance, discussion and reflection, their confidence in using and understanding the varieties of language available to them and their appropriateness for particular purposes and contexts' (1989b, p. C1) and

> The needs of individual children will often only be met by appropriate, timely and sensitive intervention by teachers. Planning for support and advice relates closely to classroom management, time planning, awareness of children's needs and the capacity to select within a range of teaching roles. (1989b, p. C1)

A little of this sort of thing goes a long way. The guidelines also include some examples of activities and tasks which are far more likely to be of help to teachers. The examples are generally ambitious, in terms both of their expectations of children and of the resources required. They begin to make clear the breadth and depth of work in English that the National Curriculum aspires to cover.

At about this time, when the details of the new curriculum were being published and discussed, it was possible to meet headteachers in a number of schools who seemed to believe that since they had always emphasized the 'three Rs' in their curriculum they would need to do little to meet the requirements of the core National Curriculum for English. Clearly they remained quite unaware that a language curriculum based on progress through a reading scheme, through individual work-books of English exercises in comprehension and grammar, and on a weekly spelling test, was no longer adequate. Compared to this traditional fare the National Curriculum for English represents little short of a revolution. Its success may hinge on how far it is possible to design assessments sensitive enough to reach the detailed aims of the programmes of study, and how far teachers are willing and able to put the programmes of study into practice without simply attempting to 'teach to the tests'. If they use the statements of attainment as a glorified checklist and become obsessed with the standard assessment tasks then little good will have come of the exercise. If they go back to 'Cox', and to the thinking that lies behind it, and teach in the spirit of the programmes of study, then standards of English teaching may indeed actually be raised.

## REFERENCES

Allen, D. (1988) *English, Whose English?* London: National Association of Advisers in English.

CACE (Central Advisory Council for Education in England) (1967) *Children and Their Primary Schools*. London: HMSO (the Plowden Report).

Cox, C. B. and Dyson, A. E. (eds) (1969) *Fight for Education: A Black Paper*. London: Critical Quarterly Society.

DES (1975) *A Language for Life*. London: HMSO (the Bullock Report).

DES (1984) *Curriculum Matters: English from 5 to 16*. London: HMSO.

DES (1986, 1988) *Curriculum Matters: English from 5 to 16 Incorporating Responses*, 2nd edn. London: HMSO.

DES and Welsh Office (1988a) *Report of the Committee of Enquiry into the Teaching of English*. London: HMSO (the Kingman Report).

DES and Welsh Office (1988b) *English for Ages 5 to 11*. London: DES and Welsh Office.

DES and Welsh Office (1988c) *English for Ages 5 to 16*. London: DES.

DES and Welsh Office (1989) *English for Ages 5 to 16*. London: HMSO.

ILEA (1987) *The Primary Language Record: Handbook for Teachers*. London: Centre for Language in Primary Education, ILEA.

Marshall, S. (1970) *An Experiment in Education*. Oxford: Oxford University Press.

NCC (1989a) *English 5 – 11 in the National Curriculum: A Report to the Secretary of State for Education and Science on the Statutory Consultation for Attainment Targets and Programmes of Study in English at the First Two Key Stages*. York: NCC.

NCC (1989b) *English Key Stage 1: Non-statutory Guidance*. York: NCC.

Simon, B. (1985) *Does Education Matter?* London: Lawrence and Wishart.

Wilkinson, A. (1986) *The Quality of Writing*. Milton Keynes: Open University Press.

# Chapter 3

# Mathematics in the National Curriculum

*Peter Frost*

## INTRODUCTION

The teaching of mathematics is a major area of popular debate about education. The learning of tables and whether children can add up and take away with rapid and consistent accuracy are seen to be of central importance. Certainly, rhetoric in the media tends to create a picture of falling standards and the adoption by teachers of progressive, and even subversive, approaches. These are sometimes seen to involve an unhealthy reliance on electronic calculators. However, a number of authoritative reports and surveys of the last ten years indicate that the controversial ideas about teaching mathematics have not been as widespread as was thought in the mid-1970s, when teachers were accused of being the 'wild persons of the classroom' and responsible for a neglect of basic skills in mathematics. Contrary to the public notion of falling standards, recent evidence, including the HMI publication (HMI, 1989) indicates that there have been gains in standards of numeracy in primary schools. There is also consistent evidence from studies in the last decade that basic skills in mathematics are given a high priority in the primary curriculum. Of course, it is easier for the public to believe a headline 'UK Schools at the Bottom of the World League in Sums' than to read in the small print the results of systematic data collection about standards and teaching methods in mathematics.

The unfounded criticism of mathematics teaching appeals to lay opinion, which is a cornerstone of the political support for the Westminster-dictated National Curriculum (see Chapter 1). The introduction of a National Curriculum which is controlled by the Secretary of State originated from the perceived need for a return to basic skills. Because of this a severely traditionalist, 'basics' mathematics curriculum might have been expected. However, the presence of professional educators in the Mathematics Working Group created a tension between the political aspirations of the then Secretary of State, Kenneth Baker, and the accumulated professional advice on how mathematics in schools should develop. It will be shown here that these tensions between the professional and the political have resulted in a more complex picture with contradictions between the content of the statutory material and the lack of clarity about pedagogy in the non-statutory guidance (NSG) (see Chapter 5).

## THE TEACHING OF MATHEMATICS IN PRIMARY SCHOOLS

A major survey by Barker-Lunn (1984) concluded that basic skills were a dominant feature across the primary curriculum in the junior years. Reports dating from the beginning of the last decade (HMI, 1978), ORACLE (Galton, Simon and Croll, 1980), Cockroft (1982), have shown that, for many teachers, there is a preference for a more traditional approach to the teaching of mathematics. The HMI primary survey of 1978 (DES, 1978) used a mixture of standardized tests, discussion and observation for its assessments. It found that, far from teachers neglecting basic skills, children were practising them, in isolation, often for about half the time. The application of number work to everyday situations was found to be poor. Generally, standards were 'disappointing', especially for more 'able pupils' (*sic*). There was too much reliance on work cards and commercial schemes, with not enough blackboard work involving the class. They advised that 'challenging questions and quick recall of number facts are essential to maths learning and often require lively contact between the teacher and a group of children' (DES, 1978).

HMI found no widespread use of informal, exploratory methods. The norm was a 'didactic' style of teaching, but still lacking in the class and group discussion of mathematics.

Similarly, a questionnaire set up by the Classroom Interaction Project (CIP, 1979) found little sign of the widespread use of 'progressive methods'. Considerable time was spent on number work, very little on shape and most time was spent on written recording. Most of the activities were desk-based with little evidence of practical experience. There was little integration and 82 per cent of schools used commercial schemes as a core. Most frequently used as a teaching resource was the blackboard and textbooks.

The Assessment of Performance Unit (APU, 1980, 1981) published two reports involving both written and, later, practical tests. These were given to a substantial sample of 11-year-olds. The reports suggest that those tested appeared to have grasped some basic skills and concepts but had problems when these became too complex. Applying mathematics to unfamiliar situations was a particular weakness identified. The often quoted example is that only a quarter of those tested answered correctly a question about batting averages in cricket, though when presented with the question in a simpler form, over half got the right answer. Of course, it would now be interesting to have an analysis by gender of the responses to this question.

After much debate and quite a few surveys and reports to act as back-up, it has emerged that it is not so much that teachers refuse to teach 'the basics', as that they teach them in a restrictive and limited way. Surveys have shown that children can often recall the basic four rules of number and functions with simple place value, but cannot relate these to other situations, particularly those in the everyday world (see Cockcroft, 1982; APU, 1980, 1981; HMI 1978). The frequent model for teaching mathematics has been that children follow a commercial scheme from cover to cover and little else, despite the fact that various studies have suggested that this is a poor strategy, including HMI (1978, 1985). Cockcroft (1982) and Hughes (1987). HMI (1989) comments on the dangers of teachers becoming attached to the newer, more comprehensive schemes and reluctant to deviate from them. HMI comments, 'There is little evidence to suggest that heavy reliance on routine sessions of mathematics based on text books and published work cards resulted in the most effective learning' (HMI, 1989, p. 24).

Other studies have also provided data to suggest that some popular schemes are poorly matched to pupils in areas as readability, layout and structure (see Austen, 1982). It has generally been accepted in these reports that what is required is for the children to relate 'the basics' to everyday situations through investigations, games and problem-solving in an integrated context. The psychologist, Richard Skemp (1989), supported by Hughes (1987), Choat (1978) and others, maintains that children must gain real understanding by learning basic skills through exploring practical apparatus and number patterns in a variety of contexts, getting a 'feel' for number.

The Cockcroft Committee (1982) provided the basis for a new realism about some aspects of mathematics which had previously been taught by rote without children really understanding, resulting in frustration and demotivation. Interesting examples were in the teaching of some aspects of fractions, multiplication and division. Cockcroft's guidance has generally been accepted, together with the need for children to be stimulated by mathematics. It seems that children and adults are still afraid of maths. They need to see it as fun, challenging and positive, rather than sterile, tedious and negative. Cockcroft (1982) noted that some adults who were approached to discuss childhood memories refused when they learned that the subject was mathematics. The committee argued strongly against any 'back to basics' initiative and urged the application of mathematics to real situations which should involve discussion and practical work. There was also a recognition that teachers need to improve number recall, oral maths and mental agility and sensibly integrate the use of calculators and computers into the curriculum.

HMI (1985, 1989) has provided helpful guidelines about essential features of the primary school mathematics curriculum, in terms both of content and the development of real understanding and concepts. Also stressed is the need for more 'talking maths' in small and large groups. HMI (1989) suggests that this is still generally the case:

> For the most part mathematics is still taught as a separate subject in relative isolation from the rest of the curriculum. Insufficient

emphasis is given to extended problem-solving and the application of mathematics to everyday life. (HMI, 1989)

There have, however, been criticisms of these HMI documents and the Cockcroft Report for being strong on what is *wrong* in the teaching of mathematics and what is *required*, but weak on how this can be successfully integrated into the proclivities of the classroom. The failure to take initiatives in this, given the pressure of the National Curriculum legislation, may well result in teachers retaining 'the old ways'. The report by HMI (1989) notes the different extremes of performance when teachers move away from the heavy reliance on commercial schemes. There is a suggestion that successful teachers who do not use commercial schemes generally make effective use of assessment of children's performance. The National Curriculum and the new network of inspection and school advisers will need to offer constructive support to teachers about teaching methods if the lessons from reports and surveys of the last decade are to be successfully learned.

The discarding of the practical applications in mathematics contained in profile component 3 (see later in this chapter for details) from the National Curriculum orders, indicates that the road to success may be long and hazardous. The consistent acknowledgement of practical applications and problem-solving as key areas for future improvement runs the risk of becoming lost in the pressure to deliver the other distinct areas of content.

## DEVELOPING A NATIONAL CURRICULUM FOR MATHEMATICS

The Mathematics Working Group was originally chaired by Roger Blin-Stoyle (who resigned in December 1987) and after January 1988, by Duncan Graham, who was later to take charge of the National Curriculum Council. Members of the group included Hilary Shuard, Margaret Brown and HMI Jim Mayhew, and there were contributions from Anita Straker, which provided some informed expertise from primary education. There was only limited representation from practising primary school teachers.

Prior to the establishment of the working group the DES had commissioned a report from King's College, London (1987) to draw on existing research and propose a range of attainment targets to inform the group in the latter stages of their deliberations. Margaret Brown and Brenda Denver headed the team, which met for ten months and produced a report in November 1987. There are recommendations and cautions contained in this report which are of considerable interest. The report commented particularly on Attainment Targets (ATs), testing, and in-service education of teachers (INSET). It was considered that ATs should take the form of a developmental hierarchy of targets which children at any age could tackle (though there were reservations about seeing the development of mathematics in a rigid hierarchy). A system of national sampling could inform the government, parents and teachers at what age children normally reached these targets. There was a warning in the King's College Report that targets for particular ages could lead to counter-productive streaming and to teaching to the targets. On testing, the report warned of the danger of basing the effective achievement of the national targets on written tests, thereby encouraging teaching to the test. There was a clear statement about the potentially harmful effects of written testing at 7, 11 and 14. For INSET, a network of advisory headteachers was recommended to act in a supporting role for teachers and schools. Further a National Assessment Resource Bank was advocated for interpretation of results and storing practical and oral tests. There was a general warning that any system which was introduced would take between nine and fifteen years to implement fully and would be very expensive in terms of research, trialling and INSET. Failure to do these properly, it was suggested, could endanger the whole scheme.

When the working group was established it was considered that its job need not be difficult. There had been a large body of agreement on the content and substance of the Cockcroft Report (1982) which could be used as a basis. However, the deliberations of the group proved not to be so simple. The group brought together experts from industry through to primary education, where equally strong values and attitudes on the teaching of mathematics were evident from a wide range of different viewpoints. The restricted remit of compiling benchmarks and testing in a very limited time added to the problems. Members of the Committee commented on the angry debates that took place and ultimately led to the resignations of Roger Blin-Stoyle and Sigbert Prais directly after the release of the interim report of the working group and its hostile reception by the Secretary of State. The level of discussion prior to the interim report was apparently rarely raised beyond fierce argument about fundamental principles on the teaching of mathematics, along the lines of the 'political' versus 'professional' tension signalled earlier in this chapter. On many issues, compromises had to be established that were unsatisfactory to all sides. In some cases this involved the acceptance by members of the group of levels of attainment that were some distance from their own experience. Some of the primary education members decided not to resign from the group, but to emerge with as good a report as was possible.

The *interim report* for mathematics finally emerged in December (Mathematics Working Group, 1987) after months of publicity about internal squabbles and rumours of difficulties in reaching agreement about how the time allocated should be used. It was evident that there was no easy route through the maze of bench-marks and testing in a subject where there was considered to be an 'ability spread' of seven years at the age of 11. The working group showed determination to consider the whole area of the teaching of mathematics, rather than concentrating on the ATs and programmes of study. The resignation of the Chair was largely due to the scathing criticism by the Secretary of State about the limited nature of the report. The departure of Prais was for altogether different reasons: he was a radical voice advocating a 'return' to the concentration on the four rules of number, in conflict even with the other factions in the working group. The interim report did not match the philosophy of the then Secretary of State, Kenneth Baker. The report emphasized that mathematics should be partly taught in cross-curricular contexts. Although the group did not include examples of attainment targets, levels of attainment or programmes of study, there was agreement that developing mathematical understanding involved a network of ideas, rather than a step-by-step hierarchy. There was limited information on how the group would deliver age-related targets and assessment of these. It was recommended that there should be greater use of calculators. The testing of younger children should be limited to observation. Assessments should be broad, reflect good practice and enable pupils to show what they know, rather than what they do not know. They should take the form of a mathematical profile (through oral, practical, short written, extended written and computer print-out work), rather than marks or grades.

The letter of response from Kenneth Baker, to the interim report, reflected his disappointment at progress. The brief for the working group in the time leading up to the completion of its final report was set out with little potential for flexibility. Baker expressed disappointment about the lack of age-related targets to provide parents, teachers and children with a structure from which to measure progress. He indicated that more emphasis was required in the understanding and use of number. He stressed the need to determine a balance between paper/pencil methods and open-ended problems of the type available through the use of calculators. He emphasized that calculators could be used as a learning aid and to prepare for the world of work but not at the expense of understanding number operations.

Baker's intervention was consolidated by the appointment of a new Chair to the working group. In August 1988, the group pushed into rapid action by Duncan Graham, produced the report which went to the National Curriculum Council. Here the officers considered the document in the light of advice from the Secretary of State and a consultation process, which included higher education institutions and LEAs. It is interesting to note that Graham was a constant in the transfer from working group to his new role in charge of the National Curriculum Council. The notable tensions between the four agents then in the picture (Mathematics Working Group, Secretary of State, consultation bodies and National Curriculum Council) could be orchestrated and resolved by the new NCC Chair.

The report advocated three profile components (PCs) within which attainment targets and programmes of study would be grouped:

Profile component 1 (PC1) Number, algebra and
    measurement
Profile component 2 (PC2) Shape and space, handling data
Profile component 3 (PC3) Practical applications

Thirty per cent was allocated to PC1, 30 per cent to PC2, 40 per cent to PC3.

This weighting was balanced to reflect recent surveys and Cockcroft's (1982) evidence which suggested that children need to test their skills and knowledge in problem-solving and everyday situations. The greatest allocation thus went to PC3 and this indicated that, at this time, there was still a commitment among the working group to a strong place for practical work in mathematics.

Within the profile components, PC1 clustered seven areas covering the development of skills, knowledge and understanding in number, algebra and measurement. PC2 included five areas covering shape, space and data handling. Both PC1 and PC2 had been laid out in the document with reference to the TGAT (1987) recommendation that there should be ten levels within each area. The group found it difficult to provide the same ten differentiated levels for PC3, eventually listing some general features of practical applications for inclusion.

The failure to specify levels made PC3 vulnerable to attack. Indeed, Baker made it clear that he would wish to integrate PC3 with PC1 and PC2. In this way, applied mathematics would lose its priority status against the skills and concepts content of the other PCs. These aspects of mathematics – problem-solving and application – which are seen as essential by professional educators were being severely devalued. Baker's move was manifestly at odds with much of the research over the last decade (see pp. 53–54), which had emphasized the need for children to relate mathematics to everyday situations, through problem-solving, investigations and cross-curricular contexts. Amongst mathematics educators it was considered vital to retain PC3. Apart from the points made here it is seen as an essential cross-curricular component. If this PC was to be combined with the other PCs, it should be done in such a way as to underline the distinctive nature of the activities involved and the cross-curricular potential.

It was at this point that the political intervention in the school curriculum was clear: Baker was emphasizing the importance of 'old-style sums' as against the progressive oblique/problem-solving pedagogies and his insistence on more time for PC1 as against PC2 was also seen as reactionary political pressure in favour of traditional maths. In this context the need to preserve PC3 was seen to be all the more vital. Also, the problems of stratifying PC3 according to the TGAT model of ten levels was the first case of the assessment of the National Curriculum affecting the quality of its content (see Chapter 1). This is a clear case of the assessment 'tail' and the curriculum 'dog'. The political insistence upon assessment has led to an impoverished mathematics curriculum.

Aside from the political debate there were also difficulties concerning assessment. The assessment recommended by the final report was through the following means at 7, 11, 14 and 16:

> Extended tasks (up to 10 hours) e.g. group project that could involve problem-solving
> Long tasks (20 minutes to 2 hours)
> Short tasks (up to 20 minutes)

These tasks would emerge through standard assessment tasks (SATs) or teacher assessments (TAs). It was envisaged that these two methods of assessment would cross-moderate. Teachers would also be required to moderate work of other teachers. At each age, pupils would be given tests based on their target level (i.e. level 2/3 at 7 and 4/5 at 11). At different ages these would have different weightings. At 7 the assessment would be purely by extended task and TAs. The extended tasks would be drawn from a large bank and there would be considerable emphasis on teacher judgement. At 11, 50 per cent of assessment would be through extended tasks for PC1 and PC2 and 100 per cent for PC3. PC1 would have 20 per cent through long tasks, PC2, 30 per cent whilst PC1 would have 30 per cent through short tasks and PC2, 20 per cent. These recommendations were overtaken by subsequent advice from the School Examinations and Assessment Council (Halsey, 1989) which stressed nationally administered tests (SATs) as against teacher assessment at all levels right across the National Curriculum. This advice was accepted by the Secretary of State.

Following consultation and the advice from the Secretary of State the NCC presented its own draft proposals for the maths core curriculum (NCC, 1989a). Despite their greater clarity from the work of the working groups, these new proposals were severely criticized for their slavish acceptance of political persuasion, especially with regard to the elimination of PC3 as a separate component. Although NCC acknowledged that 80 per cent of those consulted had been in favour of the retention of PC3, nevertheless in their final advice to the Secretary of State it was still eliminated as a profile component and relegated to a permeating theme across PC1 and PC2 (NCC, 1989b). This was, then, an obvious case of the exercise of the centralized power of a government department against the majority of professional opinion.

The draft recommendations recognized that further work was necessary in addressing the issues of gender, and ethnic and cultural diversity. It is disappointing that these areas will not be addressed until other core and foundation subjects are in place. Recognition of gender and cultural diversity in given examples could have raised the level of teacher awareness at the crucial stages of National Curriculum development.

The cross-curricular potential of mathematics teaching was severely reduced by the council's decision to provide no recommended guidelines or suggested strategies for integration. While the NSG for mathematics gives suggestions about possibilities, the present structure of PCs makes this difficult to achieve. To propose that cross-curricular guidance will be provided after the core and foundation documents are complete was misguided. By this time, teachers will have adopted their approaches and teaching style, which may well be separate-subject based. In addition, the lack of guidelines to assist teachers to move away from slavish use of commercial schemes was disappointing. The lack of detailed recommendations for the use of calculators and information technology applications did little to encourage teachers to develop appropriate uses.

## THE NATIONAL CURRICULUM FOR MATHEMATICS

The first final National Curriculum documents arrived in schools in spring 1989 (DES and Welsh office, 1989). In mathematics, the first-phase basic package included the attainment targets and programmes of study. In the summer there followed the non-statutory guidance (NSG) (NCC, 1989b) for primary schools, offering advice to assist teachers in interpretation. The form of the ATs and programmes of study differed little from the NCC draft version, although there was further adjustment to some of the statements of attainment and the examples provided. The orders for the National Curriculum for maths would seem to have missed the opportunity for a progressive curriculum. The political line taken by the Secretary of State appears to have severely reduced the importance of practical maths. However, in common with the other two core subjects, the NSG takes a more neutral stance on teaching and learning methods and avoids the validation of the political view of mathematics teaching.

The NSG for mathematics returns to the directions suggested by the working group in the report (DES and Welsh Office, 1988). The encouragement to use a cross-curricular approach, with practical experience to gain understanding, which can be related to everyday experiences, seems constructive. Frequent references to problem-solving, investigations and using a wide range of resources relate clearly to advice in the Cockcroft Report. The NSG has frequent references to teacher choice and the flexibility offered for teachers who plan carefully. There is an indication that the material does not constitute a universal strategy for the implementation of the National Curriculum but rather that it serves to 'provide a number of starting points for staff planning' (NCC, 1989a). Whilst there is perhaps a familiar danger here in that teachers may be forced back to commercial schemes for support, there is a strong contrast between the restrictive conservatism of the orders and the open flexibility of the NSG. It is possible that the consulation exercises were not, as many participants thought, a waste of time, but that they have been highly influential on the NSG drawn up by the NCC. As indicated in Chapter 1, the NSG contains the foundations of the approach to mathematics which was inherent in the thinking of the working group. It is unfortunate that the removal of PC3 (practical applications), for political reasons, has required a set of guidelines which attempt to re-establish this principle of applications and problem-solving, despite the fact that the statutory orders are designed to face in another direction.

This can even be seen with regard to the controversially discarded PC3. The NSG stresses the relationship between understanding skills and concepts and applying them. The use of practical work, problem-solving and investigations in everyday situations are underlined as key elements in the effective teaching of mathematics.

The NSG states that there will be particular reference to special needs, multicultural issues and equal opportunities in later documents (after all subject documents have appeared). There have been criticisms of the dangers of teachers adopting styles and approaches to their teaching which will at best be upset by these subsequent documents. At worst these guidelines may be ignored as teachers will have established their thinking on the National Curriculum. It is encouraging that the importance of exploring mathematics, solving different types of problems (including practical ones), developing learning skills, using maths in everyday life and working with patterns are stressed at an early stage of the NSG. Also, the reference to mathematics being fun offers optimism for teachers and children.

The structure of the National Curriculum provides a common framework for planning at the school level. The programmes of study matrix in itself is not intended as a scheme of work but offers features for consideration in the school scheme. The framework provided by the NSG for planning, implementing and evaluating is intended to inform the schools in compiling their own policy document and offers, in effect, the professional framework which the former Secretary of State, Baker, repressed.

There is a tentative suggestion in the NSG that schools may wish to use the programmes of study as pertaining to key stages, taken as a cluster rather than a step-by-step development. This does seem to provide a welcome added flexibility for planning schemes of work. It will be helpful when planning for groups of children exploring mathematics at different levels, at the same or different targets in various contexts. The inclusion of a definitive statement that planning based on work at a single level across the programmes of study should be avoided may provide a counter for teachers tempted in this direction.

Included in the guidelines are advantages and disadvantages in using various starting points for successfully developing a scheme of work. There is a recommendation that a mixture of using a general topic, encouraged by the need to consider 'using and applying mathematics', and some other mathematical work alongside is a sensible model to take.

There are consistent references to the rich potential offered by cross-curricular work in the NSG. This is also emphasized in the *Framework for the Primary Curriculum* booklet (NCC, 1989b). However, there is an acceptance that the subject form of the foundation areas creates a constraint in the direction of a separate subjects curriculum. Without actually suggesting possible overall models, various incentives for developing cross-curricular work are listed in both documents. These include: that maths can be seen in the real world; that it is a more efficient use of time; that cross-curricular work can create positive attitudes and that it provides a variety of contexts. Examples of how this approach could be applied to practice are included in Chapter 7.

## CONCLUSION

The most recent HMI report (1989) indicates that there have been a number of successful initiatives in the teaching of mathematics; particularly in the resources and teaching strategies employed and the context of the learning that takes place. Unfortunately, also indicated is the strong counter-movement to produce 'teacher-proof' commercial schemes that produce a grim rigidity of teachers slavishly following a manual. The result of such schemes is often a limited, linear development in a narrow curriculum setting with supplementary material that is either not used or consolidates negative attitudes and at best rote, instrumental understanding (see Skemp, 1989). Consequently, teachers can lack confidence in taking initiatives and are reluctant to project and control the development of programmes for their children. Inevitably, there are a number of 'National Curriculum-proof' commercial schemes about to flood the market, despite the warnings from HMI about the dangers of this approach.

Packaged schemes offer minimal flexibility and will probably do little to assist teachers in strengthening their own curriculum development skills. Using investigations, problem-solving and games in practical and integrated contexts, where individuals are able to relate understanding to everyday situations, needs to become the rule rather than the exception. Good practice has been developed but it has not been widely shared or disseminated. Advisory teachers have been appointed nationwide to support and encourage teachers, though their roles have often been unclear. The 'Prime Project' (headed by Hilary Shuard) has collected together the combined ideas and resources developed by effective teachers (these in turn are to be only generally available on a commercial and costly basis). What is required is a structure of planning and projecting good primary practice, where teachers individually and collectively can use a variety of resources, ideas, contexts and support to encourage enjoyment and understanding for the children and themselves. Knowing where to find out can be much more important than trying to know all the answers. This necessitates autonomy and offers viable alternatives within a sensible framework. Teachers need to own decisions about programmes and have a vested interest in the successful completion of tasks. Approaches for evaluation and assessment can then meaningfully refer to and relate to planning.

One encouraging feature of the National Curriculum is that it does offer these essential elements which might be implemented with constructive support and guidance. There will be a need for teachers to share ideas and support colleagues starting from an integrated framework and moving outwards. The ideas set out in Chapter 7 suggest strategies and ideas, in practical situations, along these lines.

There are features within the primary mathematics core curriculum which could swing teachers and whole schools towards different approaches. In some cases, the temptation of taking advantage of the ever-increasing number of commercial schemes, linked to ATs and levels of attainment, even fulfilling the assessment carried out by teachers (TAs) and anticipating mock standard assessment tasks (SATs) could be too great. In other cases, the identification of some kind of checkpoint stages in mathematics will encourage other teachers to access and select a wide range of ideas and resources in the form of integrated topics or general mathematical experiences. The NSG could have provided more clear and explicit guidance on teaching and learning to assist teachers individually and collectively within a framework, to develop an appropriate pedagogy for mathematics consistent with the models of good practice identified by HMI and others. Instead, there is a neutral approach with no clear commitment to resisting the new commercial schemes dedicated to the mathematics National Curriculum and its testing. The danger of the National Curriculum orders creating a narrow and basic model which is contrary to professional advice has not been avoided. The decision on which approach to adopt remains with primary teachers. The 'political' model has, therefore, not been completely rejected.

More firm direction, rather than mere suggestion, about good pedagogy in the Programmes of Study and the NSG could have resulted in more teachers starting with an integrated approach. This would involve using the fertile potential offered by a topic, then projecting the progression of mathematical activities that may support that topic work. With access to resource ideas, rich practical contexts and a clear awareness of using games, problem-solving and investigations to assist the development of relational understanding, this could still take place. Such practice, with a sound range of assessment, could move the teaching of mathematics forward within the National Curriculum.

## REFERENCES

APU (1980) *Mathematical Development: Primary Survey Report No.1.* London: HMSO.

APU (1981) *Mathematical Development: Primary Survey Report No. 2.* London: HMSO.

Austen, V. (1982) *Conference Report* (unpublished). Bath: University of Bath.

Barker-Lunn, J. (1984) Junior school teachers: methods and practices. *Educational Research* 26, (3) pp.178–187.

Choat, E. (1978) *Children's Acquisition of Mathematics.* Slough: National Foundation for Educational Research.

CIP (Classroom Interaction Project) (1979) *Classroom Interaction Project.* Glasgow: Jordanhill College of Education.

Cockcroft (1982) *Mathematics Counts* (The Cockcroft Report). London: HMSO.

DES (1978) *Primary Education in England.* London: HMSO.

DES (1979) *Mathematics 5–11.* London: HMSO.

DES and Welsh Office (1988) *Mathematics for Ages 5 to 16.* London: DES and Welsh Office.

DES and Welsh Office (1989) *Mathematics in the National Curriculum.* London: HMSO.

Galton, M., Simon, B., and Croll, P. (1980) *Inside the Primary Classroom.* London: Routledge and Kegan Paul.

HMI (1978) *Primary Education in England*. London: HMSO.
HMI (1985) *Curriculum Matters 3: Mathematics from 5 to 16*. London: HMSO.
HMI (1989) *Aspects of Primary Education: Mathematics Teaching in Schools*. London: HMSO.
Halsey, P. (1989) *National Curriculum Assessment and Testing* (letter to Secretary of State Baker, 13 July). London: SEAC.
Hughes, M. (1987) *Children and Number*. Oxford: Blackwell.
King's College, London (1987) *Targets for Mathematics in Primary Education*. Coventry: University of Warwick.
Mathematics Working Group (1987) *Interim Report*, London: DES.
NCC (1989a) *Mathematics: Non-statutory Guidance*. York, NCC.
NCC (1989b) *Curriculum Guidance 1: A Framework for the Primary Curriculum*. York: NCC.
Skemp, R. (1989) *Maths in the Primary School*. London: Routledge and Kegan Paul.
TGAT (Task Group on Assessment and Testing) (1987) *A Report*. London: DES.

# Chapter 4

# Science in the National Curriculum
*Ron Ritchie*

This chapter outlines significant influences and constraints on science education in primary schools over the last decade. This background to science as a core subject in the National Curriculum includes a brief discussion of recent research activities and the significance of a constructivist approach to science. The production of the science National Curriculum and the key issues involved are then described. The orders and the NCC's non-statutory guidance are discussed.

## BACKGROUND

In 1987, when the Secretary of State announced his plans for the National Curriculum, the biggest surprise for many primary teachers was the inclusion of science as a core subject. In most primary schools science had only recently become an accepted subject in the curriculum, and it was usually tackled in a fairly *ad hoc* manner and was often regarded as an 'optional extra'.

However, this situation was a considerable improvement on what HMI reported in its 1978 survey of primary schools:

> Few primary schools visited in the course of this survey had effective programmes for the teaching of science. There was a lack of appropriate equipment; insufficient attention was given to ensuring proper coverage of key scientific notions; the teaching of processes and skills such as observing, the formulating of hypotheses, experimenting and recording was often superficial. The work in observational and experimental science was less well matched to chil-

dren's capabilities than work in any other area of the curriculum. (DES, 1978, p. 58)

From this to science as a core element of the National Curriculum is a considerable change in a decade. It was a decade, however, that included a number of important initiatives that produced a climate in which teachers began to recognize the importance of science.

There were numerous national initiatives such as the Learning Through Science project (which grew out of the influential Science 5–13 project), the work of the Assessment of Performance Unit (APU) and education support grant (ESG) funding for advisory teachers. The Learning Through Science team produced pupil materials that provided a valuable support for many teachers who were attempting to introduce science into their classes. It also published useful books on resourcing science, developing a school policy and helping children with special educational needs. Dissemination of the APU findings considerably improved teachers' awareness of the importance of giving particular attention to developing specific scientific skills, such as fair-testing, in children. The research indicated that 11-year-olds were generally competent in generic skills like observing and measuring but much less successful in defining patterns in observations, giving explanations, predicting, hypothesizing, controlling variables and planning investigations (APU, 1983, p. 30).

In 1985, the initial ESGs for science provided fifty LEAs with advisory teachers whose work involved supporting teachers in their classrooms, running courses and producing curriculum materials. This work was evaluated nationally by Initiatives in Primary Science: an Evaluation (IPSE). The role of the four evaluators also included supporting advisory teachers and disseminating examples of good practice. In 1986, the funding was increased to cover nearly all the other LEAs.

Throughout the period the Association for Science Education (ASE) recruited more and more primary teachers and the emphasis of its activities and publications shifted from being exclusively secondary towards supporting all sectors. The annual conferences, which attract thousands of teachers each year, have provided a natural focus for an ongoing debate about the implementation of science in primary schools. In 1986, the ASE published a new and much welcomed journal for the primary sector, *Primary Science Review*.

Local initiatives have also flourished since 1978 and most LEAs and many schools developed primary science guidelines. A review of LEA policies indicates a remarkable consensus on the nature of primary science in terms of the skills and attitudes involved. The following, included in Avon's guidelines (1981), was typical: 'skills – observing, comparing and classifying, predicting, estimating and measuring, testing, communicating, critically interpreting information; attitudes – curiosity, originality, co-operation, perseverance, open-mindedness, self criticism, reponsibility, interdependence in thinking, self discipline' (Avon, 1981, p. 2).

There was far less agreement about the concepts involved in science at a primary level. Some have suggested that this is because definition of these is considerably harder; others, that content was regarded as less important at this time as far as LEAs were concerned. Some county guidelines included HMI or APU lists. Avon grouped nearly sixty generalized statements under the following seven headings: 'living things and their processes, interdependence of living and non-living, cause and effect, change, matter, time, energy' (Avon, 1981, p. 8).

Many LEA guidelines stressed that good practice in primary science involved the inclusion of science in topic work as part of a cross-curricular approach. Examples of topic webs, indicating opportunities for science, can be found in many guidelines. There was agreement in most LEAs that primary science should not be a 'watered-down' version of secondary science but should build on the natural curiosity and drives a child brings to school at the age of 5. Most assumed science would be taught by all class teachers and that schools would appoint co-ordinators or teachers with particular responsibility for developing science. Help was offered on drawing up school policies, resourcing science and in some cases assessment and record-keeping.

The process through which individual schools produced school science policies was recognized by many heads, advisers and advisory teachers to be as important in terms of curriculum development as the policy itself. However, in many schools the task of producing a written policy fell on the post-holder, who was expected to write the necessary document, often as part of an in-service course. Policies produced in this way tended to be of limited value to schools and simply served the purpose of being available when necessary for HMI and LEA advisers.

Local authorities and institutions of higher education increased the number of courses available for teachers in science considerably during the 1980s. There was also increased variety in the courses: some continued to offer the less confident teacher support in starting science but others addressed the particular needs of post-holders and some the problem of improving primary teachers' background knowledge in science.

Since 1985, according to the Science Working Group (DES and Welsh Office, 1988, p. 3), HMI reports have indicated that far more teachers now include science in their classrooms but many still lack confidence in this area of the curriculum. The main reasons for this almost certainly include the lack of background scientific knowledge of many of our existing primary teachers. This is due to the limited, inappropriate and inadequate science education most of them received at school and during training.

The 1978 HMI Report had acknowledged this problem: 'The most severe obstacle to the improvement of science in the primary school is that many existing teachers lack a working knowledge of elementary science appropriate to children of this age' (DES, 1978, p. 62). More recent research by Kruger and Summers (1988) suggested that the picture had not changed. Their research confirmed that most primary teachers they interviewed had problems with their own understanding of science concepts and felt they had received a poor science education. While all intending primary teachers must have a qualification in maths and English the same is not true of science. Many of our primary school teachers, of which the majority are women, have no formal qualifications in science and were trained at a time when science was not regarded as an important element of the primary curriculum. Many, especially girls, have used the options system in secondary schools to avoid science beyond the age of 14. Those that do have qualifications tend to have studied biology or the natural sciences. Fortunately, this situation should improve over the next decade when new recruits to teaching will themselves have experienced a National Curriculum that includes science as a core element.

The Conservative government's particular interest in science was signalled in 1985 when the DES published *Science 5–16*, which began, 'Science should have a place in the education of all pupils of compulsory school age, whether or not they are likely to go on to follow a career in science or technology (DES, 1985, p. 1). This was the first policy document to be published covering a curriculum area and the choice of science indicated the priority attached to it. It was a positive statement advocating 'science for all' that was warmly welcomed by those involved in science education. The fact that it dealt with the whole school age range and addressed the issue of continuity was particularly well received. It was also quite clear in stating that it was the responsibility of 'all class teachers, without exception' (p. 7) to include science in their teaching. The document also tackled another thorny issue that had concerned many . . . did content matter in primary science?

For many years, advocates of primary science had emphasized a process approach, suggesting that the content involved was far less important than the processes and skills used by children to explore and investigate the world around them. Wynne Harlen made a major contribution to this debate in her 1978 article, 'Does content matter?' Her conclusions, that some content is inevitable and therefore it is best to provide content guidelines which ensure breadth and balance, were echoed in *Science 5–16* and subsequently in the National Curriculum. She was insistent that the content she was suggesting was ideas, generalizations and facts and not prescriptive statements like 'separating sand and salt from a mixture of the two'. In Harlen's words, 'What seems to be required are content guidelines that are firm enough to ensure that children encounter the range of ideas and facts which are relevant to understanding their environment, yet are loose enough to enable teachers to use a variety of routes to get at them' (Harlen, 1978, p. 622). Despite this advice, content and the development of knowledge and understanding have been given far less emphasis in primary schools than process approaches that encourage the development of scientific skills. The implications of this are that most teachers have planned their science in a less structured and systematic manner than some argue is desirable. They have, according to Jim Rose (Chief HMI for Primary Schools), 'failed to capture progression' (quoted in Ritchie *et al.*, 1987, p. 1). The lack of emphasis on knowledge and understanding in the classroom has also meant that in-service and initial training has often paid little attention to the nature of children's learning in science. It is only in recent years that research projects have addressed the question of how young children's scientific ideas about the world around them develop.

In the context of the National Curriculum this research and its implications for teachers is of great significance. The Children's Learning in Science (CLIS) project, based at Leeds University, and Science Processes and Concept Exploration (SPACE), based at Liverpool, are two projects providing teachers with valuable information about children's learning. Both highlight the importance of recognizing that learners actively construct ideas for themselves and that existing ideas that children bring to the classroom have a significant influence on the development of new ideas (Children's Learning in Science, 1987; Watt, 1987). Crucially, these existing ideas that children bring to new experiences may not be acceptable in a scientific sense. Considerable evidence is now being collected that shows children hold common alternative ideas about the world that are uninfluenced or influenced in unanticipated ways by science teaching! For example, the CLIS project has found that many 16-year-olds hold the alternative idea that cold is something that can travel from one place to another. When asked to explain why the metal part of a bicycle's handlebar feels colder than the plastic grip many talk in terms of 'cold moving from the metal parts into the body' (Children Learning in Science, 1984). Because these alternative ideas make sense in the pupil's own terms and are supported by direct and indirect evidence they are often very strongly held. This particular alternative idea will no doubt have been reinforced by adult comments like, 'Shut the door, don't let the cold in'. Constructs which do not match accepted scientific ideas obviously have their origins earlier in children's education and primary teachers have a responsibility to identify and confront them.

A constructivist approach to learning involves the following: orientating children to new areas of content; eliciting their existing ideas about the content; taking those ideas seriously; providing experiences to test and if necessary challenge those existing ideas; offering more acceptable scientific ideas as ones worth testing; providing opportunities for children to reconstruct their ideas and articulate them; encouraging children to apply newly restructured ideas in other situations (Driver and Oldham, 1986).

According to Ausubel, 'The most important single factor influencing learning is what the learner already knows; ascertain this and teach him [sic] accordingly.' (1968, p. 685). Although many would argue that this approach is the basis of a child-centred philosophy of education its particular implications for science education in terms of the common alternative ideas children hold are considerable. Consequently, the validity of this constructivist view of learning is now widely agreed by the science education community (Pope and Gilbert, 1983; Driver and Oldham, 1986) although its significance has not yet been communicated to most primary school teachers. Another aspect of science education that has not been given adequate attention in the past is assessment. Few teachers have developed specific modes of assessing children's practical science activities and most rely on subjective methods that are rarely made explicit or recorded formally. The work of the APU, mentioned earlier, had a considerable influence on the quality of classroom work in schools that experienced the testing procedures used, but offered teachers little in terms of practical methods of assessing children as an on-going part of classroom work. Harlen's work on assessment, *Match and Mismatch* (1977), again influenced many teachers and encouraged them to think more seriously about the work they planned for children but most found the practical implementation of her ideas for recording progress very difficult. It was common to find this work discussed on courses and used to help teachers identify the progression involved in process skills. However, finding evidence of teachers making an explicit attempt to assess children's progress and record it proved difficult for IPSE when they looked for examples to disseminate (IPSE, 1988a).

The enthusiasm of many talented and conscientious teachers, encouraged and supported by the various local and national initiatives, means that there are now many examples of good practice in primary science. Many primary teachers have become expert at identifying opportunities for science experiences for their children within the classroom and beyond. They plan appropriate science activities within an integrated curriculum rather than isolate watered-down secondary science experiments in a timetabled slot. The science activities are planned to suit the individual needs and interests of the children and begin from ideas that the children already hold. The content and contexts used are chosen to reflect our multicultural society and to motivate all children, especially girls. These teachers provide broad and balanced science experiences for all the children in their class. The extent to which the National Curriculum will endorse and extend this good practice will now be explored.

## PRODUCING A NATIONAL CURRICULUM FOR SCIENCE

The Secretary of State for Education set up a working group to recommend attainment targets and programmes of study for science in July 1987. The composition of the group was generally welcomed by teachers, and the choice of Jeff Thompson of Bath University as Chair and the inclusion of Ros Driver, who directs the CLIS project, were popular appointments. There were a number of members with considerable primary experience, including Wynne Harlen of the University of Liverpool who chaired the primary group. The original brief was to look at science although this was extended in September 1987 to cover technology in the primary phase and three extra primary members were added to the group.

The decision to include technology proved controversial, particularly since 'design' was ignored and caused considerable problems when the Design and Technology Working Group was formed in August 1988 to report on the whole 5–16 age range. The then Secretary of State, Kenneth Baker, seemed to share a common misconception that technology was merely applied science rather than a broader area of experience that draws on a number of disciplines. Fortunately, this misconception was recognized fairly soon. In the event, the technology section of the science report was not followed up and simply provided useful material for the design and technology group to use.

The construction of a National Curriculum for science was a daunting task for the group. On reflection, some have seen the task as similar to trying to do a jigsaw without a picture (West, 1988). One of the dilemmas of approaching a National Curriculum in the way the Secretary of State required was that essential thinking about the structure of the whole curriculum did not occur and so each 'subject' area had to produce its own view of the overall curriculum. This made co-ordination and integration of different curriculum elements extremely difficult.

The Science Group published an interim report in November 1987 (Science Working Group, 1987). This indicated their initial thinking, outlining the contribution of science to the overall curriculum; knowledge, skills, understanding and aptitudes (later changed to attitudes) expected by the ages of 7, 11, 14 and 16; and programmes of study that would ensure continuity from 5 to 16.

The group had obviously been hard pressed to produce this report in the time available and in places it was fairly 'raw'. As the Science Group, along with Mathematics, were the first groups to be established they were also working in uncharted waters and trying to balance the political predilections of the Secretary of State with the educational hopes of the profession. However, it was clear that the group was starting from the widely accepted aims of science education (from *Science 5–16* (DES, 1985, pp. 3–5)) and basing their approach on existing good practice. The philosophy articulated in this report was widely commended by the science education community and statements about the need for science experiences to be 'based on real experience' and developed as 'part of the whole curriculum' (1985, p. 6) were close to the heart of those who had been advocating such an approach for many years. The child was seen as 'the agent of his or her own learning' (p. 8) and the scientific process as the 'holistic development of skills and ideas in a way that is enhanced by the development of positive attitudes to learning' (p. 8). The model of science education was similar to that which informed many LEA and school guidelines on primary science. The process/content issue was tackled in the way Harlen had advocated in 1978 and science education was seen to require a balance between, and integration of, process and appropriate content.

Unfortunately, the practical implementation suggested exposed a classic dilemma between theory and practice and was not so well received. The report included what to many appeared to be a prescribed syllabus which seemed to contradict the group's espoused theoretical approach. The theory was firmly rooted in the best traditions of primary science but the practice seemed to be based on secondary school laboratory practice. This response, while not shared by all, was clearly articulated in an aptly titled article in the *Times Educational Supplement* (29 April 1988) by Beryl Pankhurst, 'Thinking backwards?'

Between the publication of this report and its final report the group consulted widely with interested parties. However, it seemed to many that the group was not having enough time to do the job properly and that the construction of a National Curriculum at the weekends and part-time by very busy individuals with other commitments was inappropriate. Surely something as important as this deserved adequate funding to allow secondment of those involved.

The group's final report *Science for Ages 5–16* (DES and Welsh Office, 1988a) was published in August 1988 and the consultation period was to last until the end of October. This document was structured in a better way than the first and provided what was widely agreed to be an excellent overview of the nature of school science. (This broad perspective was inevitably lacking in the final orders that were circulated to all teachers although it re-emerged in the NCC's non-statutory guidance; see p. 84.) In the report's own words,

> We show how we see the acquisition of knowledge and understanding as inextricably linked with the development of investigative skills and practical work, and with learning to communicate effectively . . . We also stress the importance we attach to the development of appropriate attitudes. (1988a, p. 4)

The report said very little about methodology and how the curriculum should be implemented but it did clearly endorse a constructivist approach:

> In their early experiences of the world, children develop ideas which enable them to make sense of things that happen around them. A child brings these ideas to the classroom or laboratory, and the aim of science education is to adapt or modify these original ideas to give them more explanatory power. Viewed from this perspective, it is important that we should take the child's initial ideas seriously so as to ensure that any change or development of these ideas, and the supporting evidence for them makes sense and, in this way, become 'owned' by the child. (1988a, p. 7)

The report recommended four profile components: exploration and investigation (covering skills and processes); knowledge and understanding; communication; science in action (secondary stage only). The communication component surprised many but it was generally endorsed as an important element of science education. This and the first profile component also prioritized group and co-operative work which found favour with most primary teachers. However, many felt that communication was a cross-curricular aspect which should be (and in the event has been) dealt with in a more integrated way.

The group outlined programmes of study related to twenty-two attainment targets (sixteen linked to knowledge and understanding and two each to exploration and investigation, communication and science in action). The content was predictable and covered much of the content previously compiled by the APU and listed in the interim report. It was an improvement on the interim report and organized in a more carefully thought-through way although anomalies and inaccuracies were still apparent. The influence of various pressure groups could be clearly identified in these programmes including for example, the earth science (attainment target 8) and health education (attainment target 2) lobbies. Information technology was treated as a separate programme of study which dealt with information transfer. This was a disappointment to those who hoped for a broader, more integrated, treatment.

The programmes of study were listed together in the report and provided what was for many its most important section. These programmes, which indicate in broad terms the learning experiences the pupils should have, were advocated by several members of the group and others, in talks and articles (Ovens, 1989; Harlen, 1989) as the aspect of the National Curriculum with which teachers should be most concerned when planning their teaching programmes. This was seen as a way of avoiding an assessment-led curriculum based on attainment targets while ensuring continuity and progression.

Harlen hoped that the report would have, 'dispelled the fears of those for whom the words "National Curriculum" send a chill down the spine and conjure up visions of children being required to do the same things at the same time' (Harlen, 1988, p. 2). She went on to insist that the curriculum did not prescribe specific activities and that teachers had the flexibility to plan and organize science in their own individual way, within the framework provided.

The attainment targets are overall statements of objectives which children should meet as a result of following the programmes of study. It is these attainment targets which will be assessed. The report itself offered teachers little guidance about how assessment could be dealt with in the classroom and added little to the approach outlined in TGAT. It did however recommend that 70 per cent of the assessment required should be internal teacher assessment as opposed to standard assessment tasks (SATs). The intention was that the majority of the assessments made of children's learning in science would be made at the discretion of teachers, using methods of their own choosing and as a part of normal classroom activities.

The statements of attainment were defined at ten levels for knowledge and understanding but those for exploration and investigation were grouped for each key stage. This (according to the report) was to reflect the holistic nature of these processes. The weighting of the sixteen knowledge and understanding ATs in relation to the two for exploration and investigation was regarded as vitally important by the group. Knowledge and understanding was given 50 per cent at ages 7 and 11 and this reinforced the group's desire to ensure that science is not seen simply as a body of knowledge. Their model treated processes and knowledge as inextricably linked. The report had separated knowledge in order to specify different components for assessment purposes. Within teaching, the report stressed, they should be integrated and the requirements are not only about what should be learnt but also how it should be learnt. Behaving scientifically was seen as being as important as learning about science.

While not universally welcomed, the group's report gained the support of the majority of the science education community as a result of the then Secretary of State Baker's response. This was so contentious that it served to unite professional views in opposition. He was very happy about the ATs related to knowledge and understanding, broadly accepted the programmes of study suggested but had considerable reservations about the other profile components, the weightings suggested and the lack of unique statements of attainment for the ATs related to exploration and investigation. He also wished to see the ATs related to exploration, communication and science in action combined with those for knowledge and understanding. This was seen as political interference in the nature of scientific education. Baker was trying to enforce a retrogressive view of science as simply facts. Even more controversially, he proposed a two-tier approach to science in key stage 4. This contradicted the working group's aim of offering a balanced science curriculum to all children up to the age of 16. The Secretary of State proposed a key stage 4 option which covered a narrower range of attainment targets and would allow certain pupils to spend less time on science.

In the light of these comments, the consultation exercise produced a much more supportive response to the report than might otherwise have been the case. Over 2,500 responses were received from LEAs, organizations, institutions, schools and individuals. Only 10 per cent of respondents supported the Secretary of State's desire to reduce the number of profile components and 80 per cent were against combining attainment targets for exploration etc. with those for knowledge and understanding (NCC, 1988, pp. 11–14). There was concern that combining attainment targets in the way the Secretary of State suggested would provide a model of science education that emphasizes knowledge rather than one that recognizes a necessary balance between process and knowledge. The programmes of study were supported by over three-quarters of the respondents. The greatest consensus (90 per cent) was evident in respondents' views that pupils with special needs should have access to the science curriculum (NCC, 1988).

Analyses of the report appeared in the educational press (Ovens, 1989). These raised some fundamental issues which were considered to have been dealt with inadequately in the report. Firstly, the implications for cross-curricular work if science is isolated as a separate subject – it is not easy to relate the reports on the three core subjects, and the link with foundation subjects is not explicit. In particular the identified areas of content are not easily linked with humanities. Secondly, the difficulties of making the report 'accessible' to non-specialists: the language and structure is not teacher-friendly and assumes considerable familiarity with aspects and issues of science education. A third issue which raised concern was the risk of separating out the elements of science education in a way which contradicts an holistic approach – some teachers may opt for delivering specific attainment targets in isolation. Fourthly, commentators noted scientifically incorrect statements of attainment – examples of these include, 'Unchanging particles called atoms' (p. 31) (particles are constantly changing), 'Friction is a force between surfaces which transfers energy by heating' (p. 41) (energy is not transferred by friction). A fifth issue concerned the nature of science education implied by one attainment target for exploration and sixteen for knowledge and understanding – a first reaction of some primary teachers was to assume that this required children to be given lots of information through a didactic approach. The argument about whether the report provided a prescribed syllabus that would lead to a watered-down secondary approach to science in the primary school or a flexible framework which would allow the best traditions of primary science to flourish continued unresolved.

## THE NATIONAL CURRICULUM COUNCIL CONSULTATION REPORT

The National Curriculum Council (NCC) published its consultation report, which was the basis for the draft order that went before Parliament, in December 1988 (NCC, 1988). It included some significant changes to the working group's recommendations. The orders specifying the science attainment targets and programmes of study have now become statute. There are two science profile components for reporting purposes: exploration of science; and knowledge and understanding. The first has been developed as a progression in the abilities to plan, carry out, interpret results and findings, draw inferences and communicate exploratory tasks and experiments. The working group's prioritization of group work has been excluded. The communication component has been conflated into the other two components. The weightings involved in the profile components are 50 per cent for each at key stage 1 and 45 per cent exploration, 55 per cent knowledge and understanding at key stage 2.

The following attainment targets have been included for the first two key stages:

| *Attainment targets (ATs)* | *Weighting (non-statutory – from Science for Ages 5 to 16)* |
|---|---|
| 1 Exploration of science | Regarded as essential part of any science activity |
| 2 The variety of life | 3 |
| 3 Processes of life | 3 |
| 4 Genetics and evolution | 2 |
| 5 Human influences on the Earth | 1 |
| 6 Types and uses of materials | 3 |
| 9 Earth and atmosphere | 3 |
| 10 Forces | 1 |
| 11 Electricity and magnetism | 2 |
| 12 Information technology | 1 |
| 13 Energy | 3 |
| 14 Sound and music | 1 |
| 15 Using light | 1 |
| 16 The Earth in space | 1 |

The programmes of study, which were very similar to those recommended by the working group, are listed in the report, linked to the ATs. Regrettably this changed when the orders were published and reached schools. The programmes of study were hidden at the back of the document and all merged into one programme for each key stage. The aspirations of those who hoped the programmes of study would be the most important element in the National Curriculum were thwarted. The attainment targets for exploration and knowledge and understanding have discrete statements of attainment at ten levels.

At key stage 4 two models are offered, one offering a balanced science course and another (Model B) that is less comprehensive and is intended for special cases such as talented musicians who will spend less time on science. This has caused considerable concern amongst secondary teachers who fear it will mean that fewer girls will take science options after the age of 16. This concern has been countered by the stated intention of the DES to monitor the number of pupils taking the Model B option.

The NCC report bears an uncanny resemblance to that requested by the Secretary of State Baker and criticized by so many respondents during the consultation process. It left many teachers feeling cynical about the nature of 'consultation' and confirmed the view many held that the politicians would make crucial decisions despite the reasoned arguments of the profession. It was felt that an anti-progressive view of school science was being enforced by political power against professional consensus.

Jeff Thompson (Chair of the Science Working Group) suggested in a talk to the Association of Science Education (ASE) in Birmingham (January 1989) that the new ATs are richer than the original. However, he went on to say that the new proposals, based on two profile components, produced 'a dismal image of science that is to be regretted'. Generally he was satisfied with how much of the original report had been accepted but disappointed by 'opportunities lost'. In particular, the principle of universality in terms of balanced science for all has disappeared.

The NCC report included none of the valuable material on the nature of science education that was in the original report and nothing about methodology, the nature of children's learning in science and little about special needs, equal opportunities and assessment. However, all of these areas are covered by the NCC's non-statutory guidance (see p. 84).

The document which eventually arrived in schools in April 1989 was significantly different from that recommended by the working group. The job of unpicking what has been produced and finding a creative way of implementing it that does not cause teachers to lose sight of good primary practice is now the enormous task facing primary teachers. Many believe it is possible. Jeff Thompson is still optimistic and advocates the exploitation of attainment targets by teachers as 'bricks' for constructing a teaching scheme which best serves the needs of the children they teach. He sees the cross-curricular aspects of 'subjects', like communication, as the cement that holds the whole curriculum together. This positive approach is one that the profession now needs to adopt if the national curriculum for science is to benefit children.

The task for teachers was considerably helped by the publication of *Science: Non-statutory Guidance* in June 1989 (NCC, 1989). This material included much of the original Science Working Group's report. There were six sections: introduction to science; constructing a scheme of work; science in the primary school; exploration of science; the earth sciences component; using attainment target 17 – the nature of science (key stages 3 and 4). Further guidance about approaches to science for pupils with special educational needs will also be published by the NCC. The School Examinations and Assessment Council (SEAC) will be offering guidance on assessment and record-keeping in science. The initial guidance was welcomed by teachers and provided valuable support, especially for primary teachers, who were preparing to implement science in the National Curriculum. It stresses the teachers' role in interpreting and extending the programmes of study and attainment targets and recognizes the need to review and refine them in the light of experience, technological advance and curriculum development. The links between the core subjects are made more explicit in the guidance, and the emphasis on communication evident in the earlier reports is re-established. In this way, science provides a good example of political interference in the orders being rectified by the professional advice of the non-statutory guidance.

A clear rationale for science within the curriculum is offered detailing the understanding of key concepts for application in other areas; the use of scientific methods of investigation to solve problems; appreciating the contribution science makes to society; the contribution that learning in science makes to personal development; appreciating the powerful but provisional nature of scientific knowledge and explanation: and giving students access to careers in science and design and technology (NCC, 1989, p. A4). The constructivist approach to learning science, first advocated in the working group's report, is restated in almost identical terms (NCC, 1989, p. A7).

There is a list of attitudes and personal qualities that bears considerable similarity to the list included earlier in this chapter: curiosity; respect for evidence, willingness to tolerate uncertainty; critical reflection; perseverance; creativity and inventiveness; open-mindedness; sensitivity to the living and non-living environment; co-operation with others (1989, p. A8).

The section that deals with teaching science stresses the flexibility available to teachers and reassuringly identifies the programmes of study as 'the main planning tool' (1989, p. A9). This again revisits the approach advocated by the working group. Teachers are encouraged to 'take account of ethnic and cultural diversity within their school population and society at large' (1989, p. A10). Cultural diversity is seen as providing a richness to the curriculum and the contribution of different cultures to scientific enterprise is detailed. The effect of learning contexts on pupils' performances is stressed and issues relating to gender and sex stereotyping are addressed.

Constructing a scheme of work is seen as a task to be dealt with at a school level so that the written statements of the work planned reflects a whole-school approach to teaching and learning. It is suggested that teachers should no longer plan work in isolation but operate within an agreed school policy and collaborate with each other. Topics, themes, projects and a separate subject approach are all acceptable ways of delivering the National Curriculum and the decision about the most suitable approach is one for individual schools and teachers.

An excellent section on science in the primary school includes a detailed case study on a specific activity 'making and investigating a windmill'. It is, however, surprising that a task with such a strong design and technology content was chosen. Despite this the context for the work and possible approaches are carefully analysed and the links with the other core areas of the curriculum made explicit. Considerable help is offered to the less confident teacher in terms of appropriate questions, differentiation and ways of developing the activity further.

The crucial importance of attainment target 1 'Exploration of science' is reinforced by the next section of the non-statutory guidance. This offers teachers help in understanding the inextricable links between practical investigations and the development of knowledge and understanding. It stresses that the attainment targets covering knowledge and understanding should not be restricted to non-practical work. The two elements are 'not in any sense separable in the teaching programme'. The following characteristics of investigative work are detailed: defining the task; observing and hypothesizing; planning and refining; carrying out; communicating and keeping a record; deciding what the results mean (NCC, 1989, p. D2). Progression in exploration of science through the key stages is outlined in terms of context, concepts, using variables, communicating, interpreting, and examples of explorations and investigations (1989, p. D6).

Earth sciences, a new area for most secondary science teachers, is given particular attention in the next section of the NSG, where examples are discussed. Contexts familiar to primary teachers, such as sand and water play, the use of construction kits, visits to beaches, farms and churches and work on the weather and seasonal changes are included (1989, p. E5).

The final section of the initial set of guidelines deals with attainment target 17, 'The nature of science'. Although this is not a required element of primary work it does offer interesting background information. It explores a variety of teaching strategies, like the use of drama, which have considerable potential in the primary classroom as a means of extending scientific work and making cross-curricular links. This material, together with revised LEA guidelines and commercial curriculum resources that are being developed provide primary teachers with a wealth of valuable support material to help them turn the National Curriculum into a practical reality in their classrooms. The task will not be easy and will not be achieved overnight. Chapter 8 discusses this practical implementation through case studies from two schools.

# REFERENCES

APU (Assessment of Performance Unit) (1983) *Science at Age 11.* London: DES.

Ausubel, D. (1968) *Educational Psychology: A Cognitive View.* New York: Holt, Rinehart and Winston.

Avon LEA (1981) *Primary Science Guidelines.* Bristol: Avon LEA.

Avon LEA (1989) *Primary Science Guidelines (Revised).* Bristol: Avon LEA.

Children's Learning in Science (1984) *Aspects of Secondary Students' Understanding of Heat: Full Report.* Leeds: Centre for the Study of Science and Mathematics Education.

Children's Learning in Science (1987) *CLISP in the Classroom:*

*Approaches to Teaching*. Leeds: Centre for the Study of Science and Mathematics Education.

DES (1978) *Primary Education in England*. London: HMSO.

DES (1985) *Science 5–16*. London: HMSO.

DES and Welsh Office (1988) *Science for Ages 5 to 16*. London: DES and Welsh Office.

DES and Welsh Office (1989) *Science in the National Curriculum*. London: HMSO.

Driver, R. and Oldham, V. (1986) A constructivist approach to curriculum development in science, *Studies in Education*, 13, 105–22.

Harlen, W. (1977) *Match and Mismatch*. Edinburgh: Oliver and Boyd.

Harlen, W. (1978) Does content matter in primary science? *School Science Review*, 59, 614–25.

Harlen, W. (1988) Getting to know the national curriculum, *Primary Science Review* 8, 2–3.

Harlen, W. (1989) The National Curriculum in science: key stages 1 & 2, *Primary Science Review National Curriculum Special*, 10–11.

IPSE (1988a) *Building Bridges*. Hatfield: ASE.

IPSE (1988b) *School in Focus*. Hatfield: ASE.

Kruger, C. and Summers, A. (1988) *Primary School Teachers' Understanding of Science Concepts*. Oxford: Primary School Teachers and Science Project.

NCC (1988) *Science 5–16 in the National Curriculum: a Report to the Secretary of State for Education and Science on the Statutory Consultation for Attainment Targets and Programmes of Study in Science*. York: NCC.

NCC (1989) *Science: Non-statutory Guidance*. York: NCC.

Ovens, P. (1989) The National Curriculum — pot filling or fire lighting?, *Primary Science Review* 9, 2–3.

Pope, M. and Gilbert, G. (1983) Personal experience and the construction of knowledge in science, *Science Education* 67, 193–203.

Ritchie, R. *et al.* (1987) *Science as an Integral Part of the Primary Curriculum*. Hatfield: ASE.

Science Working Group (1987) *Interim Report*. London: DES.

TGAT (Task Group on Assessment and Testing) (1987) *A Report*. London: DES.

Watt, D. (1987) Primary SPACE project phase one: an exploration of children's scientific ideas, *Primary Science Review* 4, 27–28.

West, D. (1988) Half measures for science, *Times Educational Supplement*, 30 December.

# Chapter 5

# The Core National Curriculum in an Integrated Context

*Stephen Ward*

## INTRODUCTION: TEACHING AND LEARNING IN PRIMARY CLASSROOMS

The Secretaries of State have forced upon teachers a subject-centred framework which they have been left to formulate into an appropriate *primary* National Curriculum. This chapter explores the extent to which the developments in good primary practice – children as autonomous learners within a topic-based and negotiated curriculum – can continue within the National Curriculum.

The chequered postwar history of primary education, together with underlying assumptions about teaching and learning, is now well documented in, for example, Pollard (1985) and Alexander (1984). The public image of progressive primary education which emerged in the 1960s and 1970s was one of universal activity-based, discovery learning, children's autonomy and an integrated curriculum. The public image and the private realities of classrooms are, it is now known, often different. Observational research into primary classrooms during the last decade has systematically exposed the myth of widespread idealized progressivism. Instead we have a picture of great variety in practice, as noted in Chapter 1, but with a great deal of individualized learning from commercially produced materials, teacher direction, relatively little child initiation and much single-subject teaching. Some of the sources which present this information are the HMI primary survey (DES, 1978), Galton, Simon and Croll (1980), Mortimore *et al.* (1988), Tizard *et al.* (1988) and, recently in mathematics, HMI (1989). The 'myth of the primary revolution' is discussed in detail by both Simon (1981) and Delamont (1987).

Of course the myth of the innovation in primary education was bound to be easy to expose. In retrospect, the fact that the innovatory practice foretold by Plowden (CACE, 1967) was sporadic and limited is not surprising. Indeed, Galton *et al.* (1980, p. 47ff) show how the model of teaching and learning proposed by Plowden, with its complex interaction of differentiated individualized instruction and exploratory group work, is an extremely difficult one to implement in the classroom. There was little systematic in-service training (INSET) to help teachers to work through the realities of teaching along the Plowden model and there was no national guidance from HMI or DES on the implementation of this approach.

What documentary guidance there has been has sometimes been misinterpreted. The HMI survey (DES, 1978) criticized 'topic work' for frequently being little more than children reproducing verbatim material from textbooks. This section of the HMI 1978 survey was often taken as a criticism by HMI of integrated work in itself and probably had a detrimental effect on the development of integrated or thematic work. In fact, HMI were criticizing a very limited form of pedagogy which was not central to the work of those teachers who were seriously engaged in developing fully fledged curriculum integration.

Almost without exception, the National Curriculum subject documents, at all stages, hasten to explain that, while a single subject is being presented – mathematics, science, English – it is perfectly possible for primary teachers to take a 'cross-curricular' approach. The non-statutory guidance (NSG) for each of the three subjects states, in a different way, that a cross-curricular approach can be adopted. While there are strong hints and suggestions about ways in which there might be cross-curricular approaches, the subject-based origins of the formation of the National Curriculum are overwhelmingly evident in the presentation of the statutory orders. Other general documents concerning the National Curriculum, *From Policy to Practice* (DES, 1989) and *A Framework for the Primary Curriculum* (NCC, 1989e), also suggest that the possibility of curriculum integration is available to schools. However, nowhere among the statutory and advisory material which came to schools during 1988 and 1989 is there any firm statement about the direction which schools and teachers should take in addressing this issue, nor is there a consistent rationale for an integrated approach.

As will be shown later in the chapter, the NCC's public policy on teaching and learning is systematically neutral. In some ways such an impartial stance on teaching method is defensible: after all teachers, as professionals, should be allowed to select the appropriate form of 'delivery' for the curriculum content. The position is, however, a naive one on two counts. First, the National Curriculum has been devised and presented to teachers as separate subjects, written by teams with no systematic consultations between them and offered in separate publications, each with its own set of non-statutory guidance. The overall structure, therefore, is in separate subjects. Second, to assume that content can be dissociated from method is fallacious and it will be shown that the core National Curriculum, at the level of detail in which it has been drawn up, can be properly taught only in an integrated context.

The primary curriculum should be responsive to children, their experiences and their initiatives. An integrated curriculum is desirable, not simply because it exercises teachers in weaving clever topic webs which cover all possible areas of the curriculum, but because the starting points should be what children and teachers are able to initiate collaboratively. In practice, children should be engaging in activities which are real to them and which are important to them. There is a danger that the National Curriculum could be interpreted by teachers as a Gorgon's head of attainment targets in separate subjects, each to be handled one by one through a sequence of narrowly based activities focused on specific attainment targets (ATs). ATs could be seen as objectives around which a curriculum is constructed as a set of unrelated skill-oriented activities. In the haste to match teaching and children's learning to the statutory lists, teachers' initiatives in curriculum planning could be stifled and children's initiatives in the curriculum-making process be viewed as irrelevant. For this reason schools need to take a firm decision at an early stage to plan on an integrated basis.

As has been suggested, the NCC appears to be happy to see

teaching methods continue in whatever form is judged suitable by individual schools and is reluctant to engage in a discussion of what is good practice. Much of the research literature shows that a wide range of methods are in use. There is a case for arguing that this is a time when schools should be given a clear lead about what good primary practice constitutes. It is suggested here that such practice is teaching which takes account of the priorities and interests of the child, and it occurs where children are engaged in learning activities which are in themselves worthwhile and contribute to their all-round skills and competence, but which the children perceive as being significant: where teachers and children share common goals and enthusiasm about their achievement, and where children *own* the activities and learning in which they are engaged. Teachers have learned that this occurs by engaging children in activities which are real to them, concerned with significant objects and events in their lives. To achieve this, the classroom contains resources to enable initiatives to be taken and followed up; children are able to gain access to resources and the teacher is a colleague who will provide stimulus, resources, instruction where necessary, but will also be a reflective agent for children's ideas and initiatives. The curriculum is negotiated within a context of mutual respect and excitement.

In Stephen Rowland's (1984) model of 'interpretative teaching', teaching and learning are seen as a dynamic interaction between teacher and pupils in which either the teacher or the child might provide the initiative or the stimulus. The child responds and then proceeds to some inventive activity, while the teacher acts as a reflective agent, responding to the child's actions and providing direct instruction where necessary and where requested by the child.

Teachers and children will only be genuinely committed to topics which they own. It is important, then, that schools resist the temptation to 'deliver' the National Curriculum through series of set topics which are laid down in advance, without any involvement of the teachers concerned or the children who will take part in them. This point is well illustrated by the example in Chapter 8 where the teachers at an infant school felt the need to be able to retain the choice of topic theme. In this way they could involve children in the planning and employ their own creativity in the process: the result is a feeling of commitment and ownership. The National Curriculum should not prevent the development of integrated topic work derived from children's initiatives. The ATs and Programmes of Study can be derived from events initiated by children, and primary school teachers have shown how this can be achieved to engage fully children's interests and enthusiasms. One criticism of the integrated topic work approach is that the method cannot cover the whole curriculum comprehensively, especially in mathematics. However, if the unified topic which is of interest and importance to the children is at the centre of the curriculum, any additional 'routine' or directed work necessary to complete the comprehensive curriculum will be readily accepted by the children when they know that the teacher shares their overall excitement about learning.

Rowland's model of interpretative teaching, together with a negotiated curriculum on an integrated theme is demonstrated in the following example of good primary practice.

## 'THE QUIET ROOM' AT REDLAND PRIMARY SCHOOL, CHIPPENHAM, WILTSHIRE

This example of an integrated one-term topic is intended to show how the core curriculum – and other foundation subjects – can be covered in a way in which children and their teacher are fully engaged in a curriculum project, taking their own initiatives and decisions. The practice described here is typical in the school which has a policy of integrated topic work, a policy which is strongly supported by the Primary Advisory Service in the Wiltshire LEA. Another feature of this work to be noted is the prominence of girls in the science activities and initiative-taking.

It is necessary to stress that the work was done before the final National Curriculum orders were published. The analysis of National Curriculum ATs is, necessarily therefore, retrospective. The work had not been planned with the National Curriculum explicitly in mind and would be an example of the strategy 2 planning advised in the Mathematics NSG (DES and Welsh Office, 1989a, p. B12). At the time of writing (August 1989) the final orders for key stage 2 for English had not been published.

Therefore, reference is here made to the Attainment Targets and Programmes of Study as set out in the NCC consultation document for English (1989a).

Redland Primary School is in a modern building on semi-open-plan lines. Classes are paired in units comprising two teachers and two classes in adjacent areas with shared facilities, a 'wet area' and a small 'quiet room'. The quiet room, a small area closed off from the rest of the open-plan space, is intended for reading and quiet study.

Class 5 is a mixed-age one of 9–11-year-olds (Y5 and Y6). Their teacher is Carol Hudson. The children of Class 5 decided that their quiet room had become rather untidy and needed redecorating and refurbishing in order to make it more attractive. The teacher had recently become interested in the presentation of books as part of the process of encouraging children to read. The plans to improve the room absorbed their attention, and their learning, during the spring term 1989. In this short account of their activities, the thinking behind the topic and the learning which emerged are explained. At the end of each short section is a brief, indicative summary of relevant National Curriculum ATs at levels 4 and 5 (6 for mathematics), the levels closest to the ages of the children. Of course, a great deal more learning than the core curriculum at these levels took place, although for present purposes just the core elements are noted. Also evident are the ways in which the teacher makes assessments of the children's learning.

The teacher's concern with alterations to the room began when, following the school's developing policy on 'reading with real books', she became interested in Jill Bennett's suggestion that

> Children need space where they may read quietly and in comfort, out of the bustle of classroom activity. Every classroom should have a reading area, preferably carpeted with comfortable chairs and cushions, in which children can relax with books. (Bennett, 1987, pp. 4–5)

This convinced her of the need for a stimulating reading environment. She realized that the quiet room did not provide such a context. It housed the books, but also a computer; it was drab and uninviting; books were not attractively displayed and there was nowhere comfortable to sit. She set about making the conversion into a term's project involving the children. An INSET course in primary education which she was attending had encouraged her in the ideas that a topic could provide the majority of the curriculum work for the term, offering real learning experiences to the children, as well as providing a reading environment which would encourage 'real readers'. The teacher had doubts at the outset as to whether the topic would provide an adequate and balanced curriculum, and she prepared a secondary topic based on a novel to make good any possible deficiency. In fact, when the teacher introduced the project to the children they responded enthusiastically to the suggestion and quickly provided the additional ideas which were required to make the topic fulfil the term's work.

### Initial collaborative planning

From the initial suggestion, the initiative for the development was handed over to the children and they carried out a session of 'think writing' to brainstorm their ideas. These suggestions for the room proved to be close to the ideas which the teacher herself had visualized:

tidy . . . plants . . . cushions . . . paint walls . . . bean bags (for seating) . . . drapes . . . our work . . . posters . . . displays . . . new books . . . remove computer . . .

These initial ideas were written up with illustrations, showing the children's feelings about the room as it was and offering their view of its improved state. This was formed into an initial display for the other classes to see. This work involved the making of perspective drawings of the room. The teacher was able to do some interesting direct teaching about drawing in perspective as some of the children were frustrated with their initial efforts and the need arose for them to gain an understanding of perspective and to appreciate the difference between perspective drawings and 'bird's eye view' plans.

*English AT1 level 4*   *   take part as a speaker and listener in a
                            group activity, contributing to its

planning and implementation, as well as
drawing conclusions from it.

*level 5*   * contribute and respond constructively in
discussion or debate, advocating and
justifying a particular point of view.

*English AT3 level 4*   * organize their own writing. . . .

## The bookshop visit

Shortly before this time, a new children's bookshop had been
opened in the nearby city of Bath and a visit for the class was
arranged. The bookshop had been carefully planned to encourage children to browse. During the visit the children were able
to see the facilities and to discuss with the bookshop staff the
thinking behind the planning and setting up of the shop. They
were able to match some of their own ideas with those of the
adult planners. In particular, the children were able to note
colours of decorations, seating and the ways in which the books
were displayed. Also of great interest to the children was the
range of book titles available and this sparked off a great deal
of enthusiasm for books.

*English AT1  level 4*   * ask and respond to questions with
increasing confidence.

## The bean bag search

The importance of comfortable seating had already been identified by the children in their original ideas and buying 'bean bags'
was the first step after the trip to Bath. This was done by
comparing the bean bags for sale in different shops and composing *Which?*-style reports, using the word processor, taking
account of a list of criteria: cost, value for money, filling, flam-
mability, cover design, durability. This gave the children experience of operating in the commercial world by comparing prices,
handling the variables involved and decision-making.

*Maths AT3 level 4*  * solve addition or subtraction problems

using numbers with no more than two
decimal places.

*level 6*   \* work out fractional and percentage
changes.

*English AT5 level 5*   \* contribute and respond in group
discussion, seeking to reach an
agreement on a given assignment.

  \* express an opinion using supporting
information.

*English AT3 level 5*   \* write for a range of purposes.

### Choosing the colour of the room

The children agreed that the quiet room required redecoration.
When the teacher asked them why they felt it needed changing,
they replied that the green colour seemed 'cold'. This led to a
discussion between the teacher and the children about 'hot' and
'cold' colours. They then sorted objects into 'hot' and 'cold' sets
and displayed them with a selection of 'hot' and 'cold' words.
The teacher brought in a collection of paint manufacturers' shade
cards and warm and cold colours were again discussed. The
children were very interested in these and began to mix their
own paint colours, giving them original names such as 'Magic
Cola', and 'Weston Sand'. They made up a matching game using
the different colours, finding that the easiest colours to remember
were the ones with descriptive names. The number of colours in
the shade cards proved to be overwhelming and choosing a
colour was very difficult. Several children had talked about the
importance of matching colours and how their parents had matched colours to furniture and curtains. So the teacher and the
children decided to look at the colours in their homes and to
ask parents how they had chosen them. Each child looked in
their home and, on a chart, recorded the colours of the walls,
carpets and curtains in four rooms: living room, kitchen, bedroom and bathroom, and brought the information back to school.
At this point the teacher asked the children what use might be
made of this information. They suggested the construction of a
tally chart to find the most popular colour for each room. This
produced evidence of the association between colours and certain

rooms, such as blue or green in the bathroom. By this time the children had a good understanding of the term 'colour co-ordination' and were able to define this as 'colours which blend together'.

It was at this point that Emma, one of the children, proposed the hypothesis that dark colours made a room look smaller and light colours make it look larger. 'We could test it!' was the response of the other children. How this could be done was discussed by the class. Work began on devising a 'fair test' and it was decided to make paired models of the room inside a shoe box, one room painted light, the other dark. They decided that eye-holes were needed to look into the box so that both rooms could be viewed at the same time.

| | |
|---|---|
| *Science AT1 level 4* | * raise questions in a form which can be investigated. |
| | * formulate testable hypotheses. |
| | * plan an investigation where the plan indicates that the relevant variables have been identified and others controlled. |
| | * select and use a range of measuring instruments, as appropriate, to quantify observations of physical quantities, such as volume and temperature. |
| *English AT1 level 5* | * express an opinion using supporting information. |

**Testing the hypothesis**

Work on making the models involved a great deal of problem-solving regarding types of materials, joining, constructing minia-ture furniture and making the items remain vertical. The children had to decide how to divide the box into room, where the eye-holes should be positioned, how far apart they should be, and where to put the windows. This involved the children in many scientific processes, including estimating, predicting, measuring, devising fair tests, hypothesis formation and drawing conclusions from evidence. When the boxes were finished and the children came to view them, they found that it was too dark inside to be able to judge the colour effects. They solved this problem by adding electric lights to each of the rooms. The children had previously had little experience with electrical circuits, so the teacher gave them batteries, bulbs, wires and crocodile clips to experiment with. A three-stage process of exploration and discovery took place, each recorded with diagrams (see Figure 5.1).

Two bulbs were lit from one battery, as required for the two rooms, first using three wires 'in series' and then, using four wires, in 'parallel'. The children found the latter method more effective as the bulbs were brighter and this enabled a discussion about the flow of electric currents. The starting point was one child's explanation: 'Four wires are better than one with just three wires because with the four wires it went round quicker because it took longer to go round one wire.'

Each group making a model was anxious to present the model as well as possible and took a great deal of care in the painting, disguising battery leads, decorating the furniture and so on. This was symptomatic of the children's high level of commitment to the topic and to the resultant work. The children made written accounts of their work on the models and their findings.

| | | |
|---|---|---|
| *English AT1*<br>*level 4* | * | explain to the teacher why a particular course of action has been taken, or how a problem has been solved. |
| *English AT3*<br>*level 4* | * | organize non-chronological writing in a logical way. |
| *English AT3*<br>*level 5* | * | write for a range of purposes. |
| | * | modify writing when redrafting to ensure that text matches audience and purpose. |
| *Science AT1*<br>*level 4* | * | carry out an investigation with due regard to safety. |
| | * | draw conclusions from experimental results. |
| | * | describe investigations in the form of ordered prose, using a limited technical vocabulary. |
| *Science AT11*<br>*level 4* | * | be able to construct simple electrical circuits. |
| *level 5* | * | be able to describe and record diagrammatically simple electrical circuits that they have made. |

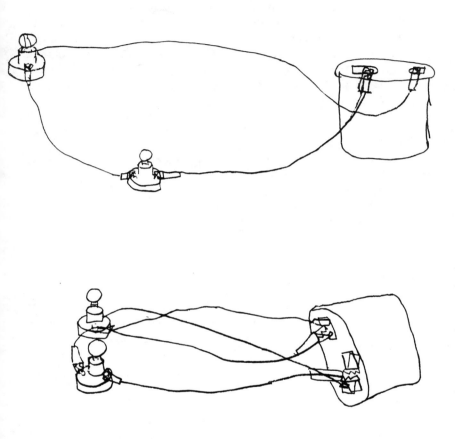

**Figure 5.1** Children's diagrams of electrical circuits, showing two light bulbs in series and in parallel

**Painting the room**

Emma's hypothesis was confirmed! A decision was taken, therefore, to paint the room in light colours as it was small and there was a need to increase the visual space. A number of colours which matched the curtains (a fixture) were selected and then began the decision-making process of selecting the two colours to be used. This involved the adjoining class and the decision-making process was recorded in a zig-zag book. The data from the voting was analysed by the class using a large book which the teacher had made, which could be displayed on the floor for everyone to see.

The quantity of paint required then needed to be determined and mathematical work on 'area' followed, calculating the areas of the walls and their relationship to the volume of paint in the tins. Predictions were then made as to which tins should be purchased. In fact the children took a decision to paint just one of the walls in one of the two colours. They had calculated that a single wall could be painted with a small tin and so this would improve economy.

| | |
|---|---|
| *Maths AT8 level 4* | * find areas by counting squares. |
| | * make sensible estimates of a range of measures in relation to everyday objects and events. |
| *Maths AT9 level 5* | * select the materials and the mathematics to use for a task; check there is sufficient information; work methodically and review progress. |
| | * interpret mathematical information presented in oral, written or visual form. |
| *level 6* | * use oral, written or visual forms to record and present findings. |

The work with the paint also involved the children learning about the consistency of paint, its properties, safe handling and drying times. Two girls took a particular interest in silk and matt finishes and constructed their own fair test to examine the differences. The teacher was unable to find any suitable reference material for children on the subject of paint and its manufacture. Therefore, having read the adult material, she presented a series of class information lessons from which the children made notes and a short report for their own books. Direct teaching of this kind is entirely appropriate where the children are aware of the context and are keen to have the information being offered.

| | |
|---|---|
| *English AT1 level 4* | * give a detailed account of . . . something that has been learned in the classroom. |
| *Science AT6 level 4* | * be able to make comparisons between materials on the basis of simple properties. |
| | * know that solids and liquids have 'weight' which can be measured and, also, occupy a definite volume which can be measured. |
| *level 5* | * be able to give an account of the various techniques for separating and purifying mixtures. |

**Planning the layout of the room**

In deciding where to locate furniture and displays the children drew up plans of the room; they had gained some experience of reading the plans made for the renovated bookshop in Bath. When they came to drawing up the plans for their own room, the teacher found that they now knew their way around a plan, understanding the various symbols. At this point the teacher referred the children back to their perspective drawings and they discussed the differences between these and plans. Following the work on perspective, the children seemed to have a good understanding of this. They went on to measure the perimeter of the room. This, of course, involved skills in measuring, but also in estimating. The teacher found their measuring skills were poor, lacking the required accuracy. Therefore, she introduced a series of practice activities in measurement taken from the school's commercial mathematics scheme. Again, we see that the relevance of this practice to the topic work makes it interesting to the children and, as they saw it, a part of what was necessary to achieve their aims. The teacher also devised a perimeter game to give the children more experience in this work. The plans were then drawn to scale. Some difficult measurements gave the opportunity to introduce 'rounding' in number; the consequent losses in accuracy through scaling the rounded number were discussed. This work on plans and scale was extended through drawing plans of the classroom.

*Maths AT2 level 6*       * understand and use equivalence of fractions and of ratios; relate these to decimals and percentages.

*Maths AT8 level 5*       * understand the notion of scale in maps and drawings.

        *level 6*       * recognize that measurement is approximate and choose the degree of accuracy appropriate for the particular purpose.

**Completing the room**

To finish the appearance of the room the children wanted coloured drapes. These were made by lino-printing patterns on sheets of material. The patterns were created from characters in literature. A booklet written by the children described the lino-printing process. Each child also embroidered a square with their name and these were put together to make a floor cushion. This involved the children in designing, choosing colours and stitches, as well as the physical skills of producing a piece of embroidery. New books were also selected and displayed in the room, which became the reading space which the teacher and the children had wanted. Finally, at a grand ceremony, the official opening was carried out by the manageress of the Bath bookshop. The children's pleasure in the room drew them inside and regular reading was well under way.

*English AT2 level 4*       * read regularly over a widening range of verse and prose, both fiction and non-fiction.

*English AT2 level 5*       * show – and be able to articulate – developing tastes and preferences over an increased range of material.

**Completing the project**

To complete the project the teacher asked the children to make a 'writing journey' for one of their pieces of writing. To do this each child took one piece of writing – on the shoe-box test, the lino prints, the paint research, the plans of the room – in all its stages of the writing process: brainstorming, drafting, redrafting and publication. They then wrote a report on how their writing had developed. This surprised the children, making them aware of the amount of work they had done. Throughout, displays had been made of the children's work. Parents were invited to a final assembly to see the room, the displays of work and to see and hear the children's accounts of their learning. Finally, the teacher asked the children to write their own reflections on the topic. Nicola's perceptions give a clear idea of what was achieved by, and for, the children:

*What I thought about the Quiet Room Topic*

I think our Quiet Room topic was brilliant. I learnt an awful lot from it. About how they make paint and how to work out how much paint you need on the walls. I think that some of the adults learnt something about decorating when they came to our assembly. My dad certainly did. He learnt how paint was made and a lot of other interesting things as well. I think that it was the best topic I have done in this school and I learnt more from it. Like how to attach little lights and we found out that dark colours make a room look smaller and light colours make a room look bigger. I also think that if I could do last term's topic again I would jump at the chance. It was hard work but it was good hard work. The whole idea of it was to make the quiet room a more welcoming place to go and read so once we had been told the question it was all hands on deck. Writing our ideas down and going to buy everything so I think that all the things we did fitted perfectly with the others like the plans, to area, to paint, to dark and light colours, to shoe boxes. It was all interesting.

| | |
|---|---|
| *English AT1 level 5* | * give a sustained account of . . . a piece of work to a group of pupils, the teacher or other known adult. |
| *English AT2 level 4* | * discuss the organization of their own writing; revise and redraft their writing in the light of that discussion. |

*English AT5 level 4*    * produce a more fluent cursive
(handwriting) style in independent
work.

      *level 5*    * produce clear and legible handwriting
in both printed and cursive style.


## AN INTEGRATED NATIONAL CURRICULUM

A dual epistemology underlies the National Curriculum: the political and the professional. Blenkin and Kelly (1981) have already demonstrated the contrasting views of the curriculum which have emanated from the DES, exemplified by the two curriculum documents which appeared in 1980. One, *A View of the Curriculum* (DES, 1980b) written by HMI, represents the *professional* view of the curriculum. HMI urges that the current developments in the primary curriculum should be sustained and strengthened and sees the ideal curriculum for primary children as essentially integrated or 'unified':

> . . . ways should be found to develop the existing curriculum by helping teachers both to frame essential processes more carefully and deepen their understanding of the skills and concepts that children should be developing in schools. Although confused in parts, the substance of their views focuses on the processes of education and their views of how learning should take place is that it should be essentially *unified*. (Blenkin and Kelly, 1981, p. 147; my italics)

The *political* model of the curriculum is expressed in *A Framework for the Curriculum* (DES, 1980a), apparently written by DES officials. In this, the curriculum is seen as discrete elements of 'protected content' with an emphasis on education as product:

> They urge the inclusion of 'common elements' – notably English, mathematics and science – which should form a substantial part of the school's work. The emphasis is on the product of education and on clearer means of measuring achievement, particularly in certain skills and knowledge areas. (Blenkin and Kelly, 1981, p. 148)

The contrasting views, then, are the *professional* one of the curriculum as an integrated whole, to be developed through increasing teachers' understanding of the educational processes, and the *political* one of the curriculum as discrete blocks of knowledge or skills to be imparted through transmissionist teaching, regardless of the learning context.

Coulby (1989) has shown that the very existence of the National Curriculum is a function of the political attempt to limit the professional autonomy of teachers, with a concerted assault on the 'secret garden' of the curriculum. The first National Curriculum consultation document (DES and Welsh Office, 1987) proposed a structure comprising a bald list of subjects, with percentage time allocations, which would be tested at four stages.

This was the political model in outline, as Blenkin and Kelly (1981) foresaw: a set of 'grammar school' subjects, with heavy emphasis on the basic skills subjects of English, mathematics and science, each to be tested at four stages. The document was an extraordinary one in its simplicity, apparently ignoring the complex work which had been carried out on the curriculum during the previous thirty years. No alternative models were proposed; the sanctity of subjects was taken for granted. Although responses were invited, these were apparently ignored and the proposals in the document indeed became the framework for the National Curriculum. The overall structure of the National Curriculum – the political one – remained intact. In order to create the National Curriculum in detail, the then Secretary of State, Kenneth Baker, saw fit to hand over the task to professionals. An analysis of the documentation will show that they have produced a curriculum which is far more complex and interesting than the model originally suggested and which, in essence, entails child-centred and integrated topic work. A separate subject framework has been transformed, from within, into a potentially integrated model.

It is important to remember the very *public* nature of the moves against teachers made by politicians, which have occupied more than a decade of rhetoric. Teachers are aware that the struggle to keep control of the curriculum is being lost. If they are easily persuaded that control of content is lost to the politicians, they may well be drawn to the conclusion that transmissionist teaching of separate subjects through didactic materials and exercises is the order of the decade and there will be a lurch backwards to such methods. In order to resist this fallacy the documents need to be read with care, understanding the thinking which lies behind them and seeing how the National Curriculum can be used to further the steady development of primary practice. The preceding chapters of this book analyse the National Curriculum documents and trace the detail of the conflicts which took place between the professionals in the working groups and the politicians, mediated by the NCC, over the details of each core curriculum subject. Chapters 6, 7 and 8 will analyse the guidance which is given to teachers in each of the core curriculum areas through the various documentation. The next section of this chapter looks across the three subject areas to examine what is prescribed in the way of teaching and learning methods and curriculum integration.

## PROPOSALS FOR INTEGRATION IN THE NATIONAL CURRICULUM DOCUMENTS

It was shown earlier in this chapter that public documentation about primary education has been subjected to differential interpretation and response. It will be interesting to see whether the National Curriculum documents receive a better fate. Much of the material is statutory, but this is not to say that there will not be differential treatment in practice and it is important to be clear what *is* actually being said. As pointed out in Chapter 1, until September 1989 the National Curriculum was a fairly chaotic paper exercise. How it is transformed into practice depends on how teachers make sense of the paper.

In the introduction to each of the working group proposals there is the recommendation that the core subjects should not necessarily be taught as separate subjects, but could be taught within an integrated framework. In the Mathematics Working Group proposals:

> Opportunities for using mathematics across the curriculum should be exploited because, as we have argued throughout this report, it is through applying mathematics in contexts which have relevance and interest that pupils' understanding and appreciation of the subject develop. (DES and Welsh Office, 1988a, Para. 10.34)

Here, mathematics as an applied activity in an integrated context is seen as fundamental to children's learning of the subject. It is important to note that the working group sees the teaching of mathematics in this way as essential, and not simply as a possible means of 'delivery'.

The need for learning in an integrated context at the primary phase is acknowledged in the Science Working Group proposals:

> In the early phase of primary education . . . children do not see the boundaries between one form of knowledge and another since they are intertwined with each other at this stage. As we have noted already (paragraph 2.6) Technology draws from other disciplines using the knowledge and understanding it needs from them to solve problems and produce solutions. . . .
>
> The context in which Science and Technology are developed is therefore very important. If this is chosen carefully children come to appreciate the relevance of both subject areas to everyday life, and to use their Science to solve problems. Scientific and technological experiences set in these contexts can, and should, be introduced at an early age. (DES and Welsh Office, 1988b, Paras 2.18–2.20)

The working group offers an interesting view of children's learning in science:

> . . . it is important that we take a child's initial ideas seriously so as to ensure that any change or development of these ideas, and the supporting evidence for them makes sense and, in this way, become 'owned' by the child. (1988b, Para. 2.10)

Here, quite clearly, is the notion of children's initiatives, and ownership, in the curriculum planning process: what children bring to science is crucial to how it is learned.

The English Working Group indicates the important relationship of English to other languages, even though other languages are not contained within the group's brief:

> It is essential that the development of competence in spoken and written English is sensitive to the knowledge of other languages which many children have. (DES and Welsh Office, 1988c, Para. 3.7)

English is seen as an integral part of children's experience and thinking, which may include, and will relate to, the use of other languages.

And the position with respect to integration is summarized by the English Working Group:

> The Reports of the various Working Groups, taken together, should . . . reveal possibilities for collaboration across disciplines that have not yet been widely recognized, with each making its distinctive contribution. (1988c, Para. 1.14)

In these early documents, then, the vision of an integrated National Curriculum for primary schools is enthusiastically embraced. It is argued that mathematics is learned effectively in the context of other topics: scientific concepts are only meaningful if they are *owned* by the child, and language/English is central to children's learning in other subjects.

As shown in Chapter 1, by the time of the production of the statutory orders, the work of the separate groups had produced large areas of curriculum *overlap*. In examining the documents for a view of an integrated curriculum, it is necessary to look beyond mere overlap to ways in which the actual programmes of study are carried out: to ways of understanding the nature of teaching and learning inherent in them.

Not surprisingly, given the form of presentation, the ATs for mathematics contain little in the way of recommendations for curriculum integration. They are largely dedicated to a detailed specification of content through disembodied lists. However, there are hints in the examples provided that the authors are thinking of activities within a thematic framework: 'Devise a survey to investigate the ages of cars passing the school by noting registration numbers; carry out survey; discuss awkward cases (e.g. personalized number plates) and analyse results', and 'Collect and display a range of charts, diagrams and graphs gathered from newspapers; interpret the information contained in the display; discuss possible headlines to accompany different graphs' (DES and Welsh Office, 1989a, p. 24).

These are activities which are more sensible within the context of integrated thematic work on 'transport' or 'newspapers'. The programmes of study, similarly, present rather bald lists of activities. There is no preface to the programmes indicating the relationships to other curriculum areas, as there is in the science document. It is evident that some mathematics might be taught within an integrated theme, especially ATs 1 and 9: using and applying mathematics. However, from a superficial reading of the statutory material teachers might be left with the idea that the majority of the mathematics which children learn will have to be taught through the traditional practice exercises. This kind of activity, familiar in commercial schemes of work, is criticized in Chapter 3 and by HMI in a report on mathematics teaching in schools (HMI, 1989). A considerable degree of imagination is required for teachers to be able to include all the items within an integrated topic and it is necessary to turn to the NSG for assurance that an integrated approach is desirable.

In the NSG for mathematics (DES and Welsh Office, 1989a) there is a clear statement of the need for an integrated approach with a rationale stating that the benefits of cross-curricular approaches are that

* they reflect the world in which we live;
* they enable more efficient use of time to be planned for;
* the contribution of mathematics to other areas of the curriculum can be maximised;
* working in a variety of contexts helps pupils to learn

(p. F1, 1.7)

These are justifications for the integration of mathematics for the sake of learning in mathematics, rather than for the benefits of children's learning overall. However, they are a call for schools to use an integrated approach.

Primary schools are urged, in their planning, to consider 'identifying the opportunities which exist for developing mathematics out of cross-curricular topic work through, for instance, the pupils' own interests or experience of the environment and the life of the school' (p. F2, 2.0).

Here is a clear lead to schools to adopt integration. It is also interesting that the NSG urges that children's interests are taken into account in curriculum planning.

The mathematics NSG document appears to give even-handed models of either integration or ATs as starting points, pointing out the advantages and disadvantages of two strategies for planning:

1 starting with a topic and extracting the elements of the programmes of study.
2 starting with an element of the programme of study and designing activities which relate to that element. (NCC,1989b, p.B12)

Examples showing each approach to planning are given (NCC, 1989b, p. B13). The advantages of 'starting with a topic' are that it

> enables 'open' tasks to be set, and makes possible an approach which differentiates through outcome, rather than task,
>
> allows for a range of elements in the programme of study to be addressed through a single activity,
>
> enables schools to begin from the point of current schemes of work and current classroom activities.          (NCC, 1989b, p. B12)

The conclusion is that an integrated approach is recommended as far as possible, with the proviso that using the elements of the programme of study as starting points may be necessary in order to achieve the full coverage of the programmes of study because: '. . . schools cannot "trust to luck" in the matter of covering the work indicated in the programmes of study' (NCC, 1989b, p. B13).

Any teaching which is not part of an integrated curriculum, then, is to be restricted to the residual elements which are not readily included in the topic work.

Finally, it should be remembered that the mathematics orders make statutory the 'using and applying of mathematics' (ATs 1 and 9), with an overall weighting of 40 per cent. For this to be achieved outside a real-life or cross-curricular context is hardly possible. The learning of mathematics within an integrated curriculum is, therefore, an inevitable consequence of adequate implementation of the mathematics orders.

If in the mathematics document it is necessary to turn to the NSG for a clear indication of the need for an integrated curriculum, in the science document this is certainly not the case. The very items in the ATs for 'exploration of science' strongly suggest the need for an integrated context and for the employment of children's initiatives:

Level
1  observe familiar materials and events in their immediate environment, at first hand using their senses.
2  ask questions and suggest ideas of the 'how', 'why' and 'what will happen if' variety.
3  formulate hypotheses.

4 raise questions in a form that can be investigated.
5 use concepts, knowledge and skills to suggest simple questions and design investigations to answer them. (DES and Welsh Office, 1989c)

It is difficult to see how any of these could be sensibly achieved in a context other than an integrated one in which children are negotiating ideas and activities with their teachers, in the way discussed in the 'quiet room' example earlier in this chapter.

The inevitability of integration in the implementation of the science curriculum is even stronger in the programmes of study. These are prefaced by well-developed suggestions about scientific activities taking place within the context of real-life activities which imply links with other curriculum areas.

> **Communication:** throughout their study of science, children should develop and use a variety of skills and techniques involved in obtaining, presenting and responding to information. They should also have the opportunity to express their findings and ideas to children and their teacher, orally and also through drawings, simple charts, models, actions and the written word. (DES and Welsh Office, 1989c, key stage 1 p. 65)

> **Communication:** children should have the opportunities to continue to develop and use communication skills in representing their ideas and in reporting their work to a range of audiences, including children, teachers, parents and other adults. . . . Children should be given the opportunity to participate in small group discussions and they should be introduced to a limited range of books, charts and other sources from which they gain information. (1989c, key stage 2, p. 68)

Both these paragraphs might well have been included in the English orders and demonstrate a clear case for integration between English and science.

In the science NSG there is an even more explicit approach to three-subject integration. In fact, unlike the other two curriculum documents, the science NSG offers a special section on 'Science in the Primary School', the central feature of which is an example of a topic on making a windmill. This is given in some detail (C8–13) and includes a chart showing lists of attainment targets for each of mathematics and English in the proposed topic (C9–10). There can be no doubt here that the authors of the document see scientific activities within an integrated curriculum. The attention given to science in the primary school is particularly interesting and is as far as the NSG could go in specifying an integrated primary curriculum from within the boundaries of the science discipline.

There is relatively little explicit reference to cross-curricular integration in the statutory orders for English, although a reference to this in the programme of study for speaking and listening is included:

> All activities should . . . draw on examples from across the curriculum, and in particular those existing requirements for mathematics and science which refer to use of spoken language and vocabulary, asking questions, working in groups, explaining and presenting ideas, giving and understanding instructions. (DES and Welsh Office, 1989c, p. 13)

However, as in the science and mathematics orders, many of the activities in the programmes of study imply an integrated approach because they require some context if they are to take place:

> development of speaking and listening skills, both when role-playing and otherwise – when describing experiences, expressing opinions, articulating personal feelings, and formulating and making appropriate responses to increasingly complex instructions and questions. (DES and Welsh Office, 1989c, speaking and listening key stage 1, p. 13)

> securing responses to visual and aural stimuli, eg. pictures, television, radio, computer, telephone, making use of audio and visual recordings as appropriate. (DES and Welsh Office, 1989c, speaking and listening key stage 1, p. 14).

Further, the notion of negotiated learning is inherent in 'collaborative planning in a way which requires pupils to speak and listen; discussion of their work with other pupils and the teachers; collaborative and exploratory play' (DES and Welsh Office, 1989d, speaking and listening key stage 1, p. 14).

The NSG for English (DES and Welsh Office, 1989c) (at key stage 1) makes a clear statement, derived from Bullock's insight, at the outset that language is embedded in the activities of the other curriculum subjects: 'Language provides the main instrument of learning throughout the school curriculum learning' (p. A1, 1.1).

Some examples are suggested which would sensibly take place in an integrated context. At 4.11 'Speaking and listening in . . .

science,' we are given a list of suggested science activities, for example:

> making a tape-recording of 'background noise'. This can be a useful starting point for thinking about noise in the environment and the extent to which it is distracting or can be 'sorted out' by the brain. The children might look at human and animals' ears and experiment with detecting direction and distance through sound. (DC 7)

This is another example of an exciting possibility for children's activities in the context of a topic on 'the environment', or 'noise pollution'. Once teachers begin to explore the practical implications of the statutory and non-statutory elements, an integrated, topic-based model becomes compelling.

This short analysis of the curriculum documents demonstrates that an integrated and negotiated approach at the primary phase was probably envisaged by the working groups for each of the subjects. However, it must be said that the presentation and emphasis is somewhat haphazard and inconsistent with different degrees of emphasis at different points, from enthusiastic examples offered by the science NSG to the rather restrained approach in the English one. This is not surprising, considering the general lack of systematic consultation between the working groups pointed out in Chapter 1. Recommending a unified approach from within the documentary guidance for each separate subject is hardly an ideal way of designing an integrated curriculum. The documentation about the National Curriculum in general from the DES and NCC might, then, be expected to provide more systematic guidance.

At the time of writing, two general documents had been issued which give an indication of the approach to teaching and learning that was envisaged. These present an apparently neutral stance on pedagogy: an attempt to avoid legislating, or even recommending, teaching methods or approaches. This position first appeared explicitly in the widely circulated document *The National Curriculum: From Policy to Practice* (DES, 1989): 'the way in which teaching is timetabled and how lessons are described and organised cannot be prescribed' (4.3).

In the same document there is acknowledgement that the primary curriculum *might* be integrated:

> The need to cover other curriculum ground means that the possi-

bilities for developing aspects of core subjects in the context of the other foundation subjects and the whole curriculum should be fully explored and reflected in the planning and delivery of much topic work. (4.8)

This is the closest the document comes to recommending integration and certainly does not reflect the emphasis on the integrated curriculum and exploratory learning stated in the working group reports, and indeed in the NSGs.

*A Framework for the Primary Curriculum* (NCC, 1989e) is the document which, in July 1989, should have reassured teachers about to embark on planning for the National Curriculum of the need to continue with an integrated, topic work approach. But it does not.

> It is not appropriate or desirable, in Council's view, to impose any particular pattern of curriculum organisation on primary schools. Schools vary in so many respects that such an approach would be unlikely to succeed. Primary schools need to develop an approach to the curriculum organisation which implements the National Curriculum according to their particular circumstances and which will make their task of curriculum planning and implementation progressively more effective as it is reviewed and refined. (NCC, 1989e, p. 7, Para. 2.11)

While teachers are told that they are allowed to plan an integrated curriculum, there is little suggestion on how to go about this, apart from an appendix containing a survey of language tasks within the science and mathematics attainment targets. This is odd in that it is not referred to in the main text and is an inadequate model of integration. In fact, the recommendation for an integrated curriculum is equivocal:

> The primary curriculum is delivered in a variety of ways: for example, class teaching, collaborative patterns of organisation and specialist teaching. It is common practice for much of the work in mathematics, music and physical education to be taught as separate subjects. Aspects of English and to a lesser extent, science, are also often taught in this way. Some schools choose to 'integrate' some aspects of work, though the term can have different meanings in different contexts: 'integrated work' can mean no more than several tasks being undertaken simultaneously in a single classroom or work area. Alternatively it can mean individuals or groups of children engaging in a study of various aspects of a common theme. (NCC, 1989e, p. 6, Para. 2.8)

Integration is here presented in a rather half-hearted way as one of a variety of ill-defined options which, for better or worse, 'some schools choose'. This is immediately followed by HMI's criticism in the 1978 primary survey of topic work in primary schools (referred to earlier in this chapter):

> Although sometimes of a high quality, topic work more often than not lacks continuity and progression, or any serious attempt to ensure that adequate time and attention are given to the elements said to comprise the topic. (DES, 1978)

This looks like a rejection of the integrated curriculum as it is currently practised in schools. In fact, HMI's criticisms are ten years old and they reported largely on examples of limited curriculum integration, usually of the environmental studies, history and geography variety in which children reproduced sections of text books. The inadequacies HMI noted have been addressed in many schools in which curriculum integration has been seriously attempted. Kerry and Eggleston (1988) give good examples of this and it is misleading that no acknowledgement of this quality work is included. The DES paper simply goes on to assert that 'More rigorous methods of curriculum planning and evaluation will be necessary' (DES, 1978 p. 6, 2.10).

The following is even more discouraging: 'The National Curriculum is described in terms of subjects which will form the starting point for curriculum planning' (NCC, 1989e, Para. 2.12.ii).

Many primary teachers would reject this notion that the subjects should be 'the starting point for planning'. As it has been suggested here, it is far more likely that good curriculum planning starts with a topic of interest to the children and that the planning for 'subjects' should flow from appropriate activities.

The model of integration seems to be derived from 'overlap': 'Decisions will need to be taken about the extent of overlap with other curriculum areas and whether it is possible to deliver two (or more) areas of the curriculum at the same time . . .' (NCC, 1989e, p. 8, Para. 2.12).

It is only at the end in Section 4 on 'The Education of Children Under Five' that we come across any reference to the nature of the child as a learner:

> Young children often learn through collaborative, exploratory, manipulative and imaginative play, but teachers must be aware of

what underlies the various activities in which children are engaged. This will allow teachers to use the spontaneity and enthusiasm of young children to provide starting points for further work. (NCC, 1989e, Para. 4.11)

But what about the 'spontaneity and enthusiasm' of older children? Why should such an approach be limited to the teaching of 4-year-olds? The document certainly does not convey to teachers an enthusiastic commitment to all primary school children as autonomous learners.

*A Framework for the Primary Curriculum* appeared in the last days of the summer term in 1989, when teachers were struggling to carry out the dual role of ending the school year and preparing themselves for the beginning of the National Curriculum in six weeks' time. The document contains some unfortunate terms such as 'curriculum delivery', suggestive of a transmissionist approach, and 'curriculum audit', borrowed from accountancy. This language is unlikely to have encouraged teachers to look forward to an inspiring curriculum for their children. The timing and placing, in succession to a great range of other documentation schools had received during the year, perhaps explains the document's slender content and its neutral stance on teaching methods. It had been heralded as the assistance that primary teachers would need in drawing together the diversity of material which had been imposed upon them in order to construct a curriculum appropriate to the context of the primary school. The document calls for a 'common school viewpoint' on curriculum planning in each school. That the common viewpoint might be teaching to a list of ATs through exercises with no context is apparently acceptable.


## AN ALTERNATIVE MODEL FOR THE PRIMARY NATIONAL CURRICULUM

The DES consultation document (DES and Welsh Office, 1987) determined the format of the National Curriculum as a series of separate subjects. Could it have been devised and presented in a different way which would have been more appropriate for primary schools? Of course it could and, if the professionals had been consulted at this early stage, then this might well have been the case. What we have is a collection of subject-based programmes of study and attainment targets, each of which specifies the progress of the curriculum from 5 to 16, exploring the links between one stage and the next. There is subject progression, or sequential integration over time within each subject, as follows:

| *Mathematics* | key stage 1 | key stage 2 | key stage 3 | key stage 4 |
|---|---|---|---|---|
| *Science* | key stage 1 | key stage 2 | key stage 3 | key stage 4 |
| *English* | key stage 1 | key stage 2 | key stage 3 | key stage 4 |

An alternative would have been to present the curriculum across all subjects for each age phase:

| *Key stage 1* | *Key stage 2* | *Key stage 3* | *Key stage 4* |
|---|---|---|---|
| Maths | Maths | Maths | Maths |
| Science | Science | Science | Science |
| English | English | English | English |
| (other subjects) | (other subjects) | (other subjects) | (other subjects) |

This structure would have provided a set of documents dedicated to each age phase: a document for infant teachers and one for junior teachers. Of course the phasing could be shorter with, for example, separate documents for the two phases in the junior years (Y3, Y4 and Y5, Y6). This would have allowed primary working groups to devise a coherent National Curriculum for the age phase concerned, with appropriate teaching and learning methods suggested and integrated examples given across the curriculum. In this way, subject content and learning process would have been appropriately linked. What is more, a primary team could much more easily have included programmes of study for other foundation subjects at the primary stage. The presentation of the National Curriculum at its introduction in 1989–90 was through definition of the core curriculum subjects in mathematics, science and English. Teachers wishing to adopt an integrated approach at this point were left with no knowledge of the content of the other foundation subjects. This made a serious attempt to continue the development of the integrated curriculum in the primary school difficult, to say the least, and would certainly have increased the temptation for a school to treat the core National Curriculum separately from its other work. Given rather more time than was available, a primary working party could have devised a full and integrated National Curriculum with a recommended pedagogy appropriate to the primary school.

CONCLUSION

It has been shown that two views of the curriculum, and of teaching, underlie the National Curriculum orders: the first, from the professionals, in which knowledge is seen as process and derived from the learner's activity; the second, political, in which knowledge is divided into compartments and is a set of prescribed skills to be acquired. While an integrated curriculum, negotiated with children as autonomous learners, is implicit in the orders, it is the separate subject model which is presented to schools through the *structure* of the documentation: a list of ATs and programmes of study in a separate folder for each subject, with various and overlapping recommendations for practice. The notion embodied in the documents, *From Policy to Practice* (DES, 1989) and *A Framework for the Primary Curriculum* (NCC, 1989e), that the curriculum should be presented as a neutral body of content to be delivered in any way which is 'convenient', is mistaken and unfortunate. Yet again, as in the post-Plowden period, teachers are being left to make sense of a clutter of curriculum documentation for which a pedagogy has not been devised and systematically thought through and with absolutely minimal provision for INSET. Those teachers not already committed to developing an integrated approach could well be led further towards a non-integrated, 'exercises' approach by the relentless lists of attainment targets. If account is to be taken of children's priorities and interests then the starting points for learning must be integrated topics relevant to their lives and experiences. This is the model of teaching and learning which should have been recommended unequivocally for the primary National Curriculum. Unless the diversity of pedagogy in primary schools is to be preserved as a virtue in itself, there can be no serious alternative to an integrated curriculum for all children.

# REFERENCES

Alexander, R. J. (1984) *Primary Teaching*. London: Cassell.

Bennett, J. (1987) Reading with real books. In Chambers, N. (1987) *Fiction 6–9*. Stroud, Glos.: Thimble Press.

Blenkin, G. M. and Kelly, A. V. (1981) *The Primary Curriculum*. London: Harper and Row.

CACE (Central Advisory Council for Education in England) (1967) *Children and Their Primary Schools*. London: HMSO (the Plowden Report).

Coulby, D. (1989) From educational partnership to central control. In Bash, L. and Coulby, D. (1989) *The Education Reform Act: Competition and Control*. London: Cassell.

Delamont, S. (1987) The primary teacher 1945–90: Myths and realities. In *The Primary School Teacher*. Lewes: Falmer Press.

DES (1975) *A Language for Life*. London: HMSO (the Bullock Report).

DES (1978) *Primary Education in England*. London: HMSO.

DES (1980a) *A Framework for the Curriculum*. London: HMSO.

DES (1980b) *A View of the Curriculum*. London: HMSO.

DES (1989) *The National Curriculum: From Policy to Practice*. London: HMSO.

DES and Welsh Office (1987) *A Framework for the School Curriculum*. London: DES and Welsh Office.

DES and Welsh Office (1988a) *Mathematics for Ages 5 to 16*. London: DES and Welsh Office.

DES and Welsh Office (1988b) *Science for Ages 5 to 16*. London: DES and Welsh Office.

DES and Welsh Office (1988c) *English for Ages 5 to 11*. London: DES and Welsh Office.

DES and Welsh Office (1989a) *Mathematics in the National Curriculum*. London: HMSO.

DES and Welsh Office (1989b) *Science in the National Curriculum*. London: HMSO.

DES and Welsh Office (1989c) *English in the National Curriculum*. London: HMSO.

Galton, M., Simon, B., and Croll, P. (1980) *Inside the Primary Classroom*. London: Routledge and Kegan Paul.

HMI (1989) *Aspects of Primary Education: Mathematics Teaching in Schools*. London: HMSO.

Kerry, T. and Eggleston, J. (1988) *Topic Work in the Primary School*. London: Routledge.

Mortimore, J., Sammons, P., Stoll, L., Lewis, D., Ecob, R. (1988) *School Matters: the Junior Years*. Wells: Open Books.

NCC (1989a) *English 5–11 in the National Curriculum: A Report to the Secretary of State for Education and Science on the Statutory Consul-*

*tation for Attainment Targets and Programmes of Study in English at the First Two Key Stages.* York: NCC.

NCC (1989b) *Mathematics: Non-statutory Guidance.* York: NCC.

NCC (1989c) *Science: Non-statutory Guidance.* York: NCC.

NCC (1989d) *English Key Stage 1: Non-statutory Guidance.* York: NCC.

NCC (1989e) *Curriculum Guidance 1: A Framework for the Primary Curriculum.* York: NCC.

Pollard, A. (1985) *The Social World of the Primary School.* London: Holt, Rinehart and Winston.

Rowland, S. (1984) *The Enquiring Classroom.* Lewes: Falmer Press.

Simon, B. (1981) The primary school revolution: myth or reality. In Simon, B. and Wilcocks J. (eds) (1981) *Research and Practice in Primary Classroom.* London: Routledge and Kegan Paul.

Tizard, B., Blatchford, P., Burke, J., Farquhar, C. and Plewis, I. (1988) *Young Children at School in the Inner City.* London: Lawrence Erlbaum.

# Chapter 6

# Implementing English in the National Curriculum

*Sally Yates*

## INTRODUCTION

During the last few years it has been exciting to see how much development has taken place in classroom language: the practical emphasis of the National Writing Project, the move towards 'real' books rather than reading schemes and the recognition of the value of children's talk. These innovations at school level have brought within sight the vision of good practice glimpsed in Bullock (DES, 1975). As Chapter 2 shows, in 1988 there were a few worrying months after the publication of the Kingman Report (DES, 1988) when it seemed that the National Curriculum might mean a return to grammar exercises and a renaissance for Ridout and Schonell. However, the publication of the English Working Group document (DES and Welsh Office, 1988), which embodied so much that was good in current practice in language, signalled that there might be further impetus for development.

While the English Working Group reassured many teachers and encouraged them to continue their positive development, such ideas may well have been discouraged by the publication in the summer of 1989 of the statutory orders for key stage I in English. These are a bald statement of Attainment Targets (ATs) and Programmes of Study and some teachers have been tempted to replace good practice with strings of activities drawn up in order to meet the ATs of the National Curriculum. There is a danger that projects will be chosen, at LEA level in some cases, because they will be suitable for covering so many of the maths, science and English Attainment Targets. It would not be surprising if teachers were to turn to the ATs in order to decide which activities will cover them, and to plan accordingly. As shown in Chapter 5, there is nothing in the advice given to teachers to prevent this approach. There is a serious risk, then, of a return to the sort of 'progression' seen in so many 'English' textbooks: children 'do' letter-writing at one stage, and 'do' capital letters at the beginning of sentences in the spring term. It all looks very neat, and there will be some governors and parents who will be reassured by this systematic approach to the whole affair. However, this is counter to everything that we know about successful practice; counter to the spirit of the English Working Group and will ultimately be counterproductive for the children who have to learn (or fail to learn) in this way.

The non-statutory guidance (NSG) (NCC, 1989) arrived in schools at the very end of the summer term 1989, for many schools far too late to include in any staff development programme for the first cohort of key stage I. Yet it contains a wealth of suggestions for planning schemes of work which would counter this minimalist approach and enrich the English curriculum. Chapter 2 details the theoretical twists and turns in the production of the various documents for English. This chapter examines what is needed in practical terms if the progress made in language in classrooms is to continue. The examples of classroom practice given are drawn from the author's experience as an advisory teacher and lecturer in teacher education.

## DEVELOPMENT STRATEGIES

What is needed if teachers are to retain the strengths of previous practice and develop in areas of weakness, in order to deliver a sound curriculum for English, is a review and evaluation of current practice, in relation to the requirements of the National Curriculum. One way of tackling this, which has proved successful, is to have teachers working in groups to plan a term's topic around a chosen theme, as they would usually do. In one particular INSET exercise it took this form:

As part of an exercise in familiarization with the National Curriculum, groups of teachers were asked to plan a project for a given group of children, based on a particular starting point, for example, a class of Y4 (second-year junior) children exploring the history of the school building, as part of the centenary celebrations, or a Y1 (middle infant) class working on a survey of wildlife in and around the school, including the pond. The groups produced web diagrams to record the results of their initial brainstorming which showed a range of activities across the curriculum. They were then asked to look at the Programmes of Study and ATs for English, science and mathematics and to record which ATs could be reached through the particular topic they had planned.

At this stage, the groups were asked some questions to help them review what they had done and refer to the aspects of the National Curriculum which were not being covered in the planned term's work.

- Besides the current topic, in any class there are a number of other activities throughout the year through which language can be developed. The groups were asked which activities outside the topic might also relate to the National Curriculum: for example, writing journals, playing in a shop or office set up in an infant class, keeping reading records/logs, visiting the library, or celebrating particular festivals.
- It would neither be possible nor desirable to deliver the whole of the National Curriculum through one topic, in one term, so what are the implications for the choice of topics for the rest of the year if all the requirements of the National Curriculum are to be met?
- There are some aspects of the National Curriculum which would be difficult to meet within the confines of a topic. How could their integration into the working day be planned? For example, time to read as an individual, with the teacher or with others, and to practise handwriting would need to be timetabled regardless of the topic.
- Are there omissions which are a result of lack of knowledge or confidence on the part of the teachers, such as the use of miscue analysis to assess reading, or the use of the word processor to revise and edit children's writing? In this case, provision may need to be made for appropriate INSET.
- Aspects of language development which do not seem to be covered at all by the National Curriculum documents may be included in the plans. These need to be reviewed and, if they are felt to be useful, retained. But it may be necessary to ask some hard questions: Is the activity itself worthwhile? Was it omitted from the National Curriculum because there are better ways of covering the same ground? The building up of a sight vocabulary of known words, for example, is an important aspect of acquiring literacy. But the National Curriculum does not mention tobacco tins full of words to be 'practised' at

home and learnt by heart before the issue of a new book. There are better ways of beginning reading. Reading good books with a clear story told in the pictures, which include rhyme and repetition; sharing 'big' books either of familiar stories or texts created by the children themselves based on the pattern of the language in favourite books are all activities which emphasize the importance of context in recognizing words, and retain high motivation and meaning.

Teachers involved in this exercise who were initially rather nervous about their knowledge of the National Curriculum and their ability to put it into practice were often surprised at how well their usual way of approaching planning could accommodate the ATs and Programmes of Study. While emphasizing the strengths of the teachers, the task also drew attention to particular weaknesses, which could then be picked up on. As with so many effective learning situations, the discussion involved in working together on a practical task stimulated broader investigations, such as the organizational factors which could more readily facilitate learning. This included the organization of the classroom and resources within it, and organization of the children's time and grouping. This was especially apparent in meeting the speaking and listening ATs; 'group work' covers a multitude of meanings, and too often means a group of children engaged in the same activity or sitting together, but working as individuals, rather than really collaborating and talking together to learn (see Galton, Simon and Croll, 1980).

Teachers also found that they were covering the same attainment target several times in slightly different ways. For example, there may have been several different types of recording chronological events, which may have involved:

—   captions written underneath photographs of a visit, arranged in sequence.
—   listing numerically.
—   pie chart.
—   a written prose account which may have required some revising and rearrangement to ensure the correct chronological sequence, as it is less visual and less immediately apparent if mistakes are made.

The teachers realized that had they started with the attainment targets and then planned the children's work to meet them, it is unlikely that such a breadth of experience would have been offered.

The importance of the planning activity was that it involved starting with current practice, assessing how well it fitted into the National Curriculum, and revising plans where necessary. The biggest danger with the implementation of the National Curriculum is that it will be approached the other way, by looking at the ATs and then trying to fit activities to them. This would lead to a narrowing of experience in many cases. As all three core subjects were covered in the task, it also highlighted the way in which one activity, such as 'timing the drying rates of different materials' in an investigation of absorbency, may involve aspects of ATs in all three subjects: they are all interdependent. The teachers involved in the planning exercise were also starting from real focal points: current interests, the environment, the strengths of the teachers involved. Topics selected for their ability to deliver the maximum National Curriculum content in the three core subjects may not be reflecting these valuable factors which lead to success.

Checklists for ticking off ATs covered have already appeared (e.g. *Child Education*, 1989), and they look very neat and efficient; however it is not possible to make direct comparisons between the core curriculum subjects, and these checklists should be viewed with some scepticism. The ATs have been drawn up by different committees using criteria relating specifically to each subject, with the result that there are twenty-two Attainment Targets for science, but only five for English. Using a simple tick chart for all three core curriculum areas, the development of language is reduced to one tick for the whole of the reading process!

## REFLECTIONS OF GOOD PRACTICE

Whilst acknowledging then, existing good practice, examining and evaluating it in the light of the National Curriculum, difficult decisions may need to be made about where there are weaknesses and where INSET is required to help develop skills. If aspects of existing practice, on reflection, do not seem to be worth fighting for, then the introduction of the National Curriculum will have been a valuable catalyst for change. Where activities *are* felt to be worthwhile, such as the production of books in languages other than English by bilingual children, it is necessary to argue for their inclusion, interpreting the language of the National Curriculum documents creatively and including them in the reviews of each key stage.

**Speaking and listening**

The speaking and listening sections of the reports caused the most controversy when they appeared, with heated debates about the rights and wrongs of using standard English. The debate will continue, in both formal and informal contexts, with protagonists reflecting their varied political perspectives. Meanwhile the children about whom we are arguing are far more sophisticated in their knowledge of linguistic variety than is often acknowledged. Judging by viewing figures, the average child is exposed, via television, to a wide range of language varieties through programmes such as *Eastenders, Coronation Street, Brookside* and *Neighbours*, as well as the range and variety of American imports. Differences in accent, style and use of language are fundamental to much comedy. Not just bilingual children, but all children enter school with a repertoire of language variants on which they draw in different social contexts (Halliday, 1978). Where they will vary is in their knowledge and experience of the form of language which has traditionally been expected in schools: standard English. If all children are to achieve high levels of literacy, they must not be alienated at the outset by teachers failing to listen to children's voices because they do not like their means of transmission. That is not to say, of course, that schools should not then build on the starting points to develop and enrich the child's repertoire of language use, as in any other area of the curriculum or behaviour. Where teachers have used role play and drama to explore the use of language in different social contexts, children have exhibited their knowledge of register (Halliday, 1978). But it is necessary, through discussion, to make explicit this knowledge, developing children's 'metalinguistic awareness': when children have acquired language as an active means of communication through speaking and listening, they begin to become aware of language as communication mechanism in itself; they realize that there are units of language – words, sentences – and that it is possible to manipulate language. It is the development of metalinguistic awareness which is crucial to the growth of literacy.

Despite the high profile of talk engendered by the seminal works of the 1970s (Britton, 1970; Barnes *et al.*, 1971) oracy has been the poor relation of the language modes in terms of developing classroom practice. Whilst most teachers keep some form of reading record, and many schools have been devising records of writing development, talk is often left to the official LEA record form, completed at the end of the year. Certainly when the ILEA Primary Language Record was piloted, the talking and listening section was the one that teachers found most difficult to complete because, teachers claimed, 'it was difficult to know what to write'. Most children have learnt to use spoken language efficiently by the time they enter school, without any 'expert' tuition, other than interaction with the significant people in their lives, and the constant desire and need to communicate with the people around them. We know that there are major differences between the way talk is used at home and the way talk is used in schools (Tizard and Hughes, 1984; Wells, 1986). At school, most of the talk is by the teacher, and much of that is questions, directed at the children, and to which s/he already knows the answer (Flanders, 1970; Galton, Simon and Croll, 1980). Whilst acknowledging that a teacher working with a class of thirty children cannot be directly compared to a parent and child in the home, it will be necessary for many teachers to plan for far more child-centred, co-operative work in their classes if the requirements of the National Curriculum are to be met.

The National Oracy Project (1989), which is now well established, will have a major role to play in disseminating good practice in oracy through the local groups of participating teachers, and the publication of the journal, *Talk* (National Oracy Project, 1989), which is free to all interested schools. As with the National Writing Project, local groups are also mounting exhibitions and will publish their own writings based on the emphasis and needs in their areas.

The emphasis in the National Curriculum on cross-curricular contexts for speaking and listening, and the opportunity to work in a wider range of social contexts than usual is welcome. The programmes of study and non-statutory guidance provide some excellent examples of ways in which talk can be explored and developed. The reappearance of drama in the non-statutory guidance is welcome, having had very little space in the statutory orders for key stage 1. Through drama, children have opportunities to use language in role play to express ideas, arguments, feelings, and to select and use forms of language appropriate to the character and situation. This in turn can lead to the discussion of how we choose and use language, and the factors that affect those uses.

For example, a class of Y3/4 children had been exploring what life was like at the time when their school was built in 1901. In a drama session they watched a group who had been working on a role play, based on the lady who lived in a large house interviewing a prospective maid. Several children commented, in the ensuing discussion, how the 'lady' had spoken in a 'posh' voice, and that the 'maid' had 'tried to be a bit posh'. Reasons for this were discussed, children giving examples from their own experience, and the class went on to work on forms of greeting, within given social contexts – the family returning from school/work, greeting a friend in the playground, a teacher, the head-teacher, a visitor in school. This revealed the children's knowledge of the effect of social context on speech variety and provided an opportunity to make that knowledge more explicit.

Other effective ways of providing opportunities for talk range from informal 'show and tell' sessions to formal debates on current issues, which are used most effectively in many junior classes. The debates are useful in that some children will find themselves having to play devil's advocate.

One teacher of Y6 children used odd moments to have children speak for 'just a minute' on a subject chosen by another child. What started out as a game, rather self-consciously played and giggly, became very popular and culminated in each child preparing to talk for three minutes on a subject of particular interest to him/herself.

However, not all opportunities for developing speaking and listening need to be so formalized. Within all curriculum areas and in the regular 'housekeeping' within the classroom there are contexts for both speaking and listening, if they are only exploited. The planning of the day's work, and reviewing what has been achieved provide real contexts for questioning and explaining, clarifying intentions and justifying choices. Working collaboratively on real tasks such as routine cleaning of the guinea pig's cage, or the construction of a fair test to find out whether light or water is most necessary to enable seeds to grow, can foster speaking and listening skills. With skilled teacher intervention these situations can foster appropriate language skills: children will learn to listen to other people's views, and explain the reasons for their own ideas. Without such intervention there is no guarantee that this learning will take place, as the following example shows.

> In one class children were working on a map of an island, having been asked to decide together where would be the best place for a lighthouse, a harbour, and various other constructions. The children were observed to call out their various choices, and then, with little or no rationale, either allowed one rather dominant boy to decide, or argued for their friend's choice, putting arms round necks of those with similar views to express solidarity! The end result was a finished map with the required features in place, but the children had not learned to listen to others and work in a constructively collaborative way. Gender divisions were reinforced as the boys dominated the discussion, and when decisions had to be made children polarized, siding with their friend, usually of the same gender. The teacher then intervened and provided a model, asking individuals what they had thought best and why, listening to their answers, asking further questions for clarity where necessary and inviting others to comment too. The children were observed at a subsequent session to work rather more collaboratively.

These children learned not only how to listen and work together more effectively to solve a task, but discussion with their teacher and peers heightened their knowledge and awareness of the criteria involved in making effective choices. Such learning is dependent on the child's being able to communicate freely with others, and where children are not fluent in English, they should not be denied the opportunity for collaborative talk and learning.

In a class in the East End of London, some children were observed working very well together, totally absorbed in their task of constructing a machine that would pick up litter from the surrounding environment. They were talking all the time, sometimes stopping to consider what one group member had said and going back to their plans, or arguing over which was the best way to attach a particular part. At times the teacher approached and asked questions or made suggestions. The result was an extremely well-constructed machine, which actually worked, and a great many lessons in aspects of design and technology were learned. The children were in a school where 90 per cent of the children had Bengali as their first language, and most of the discussion between the children had been in Sylheti. When the teacher joined the group, he questioned them in English, and they responded to him in English, searching for the way to explain to him what they were doing and why, demonstrating to him at times so that he could provide the language, and then nodding and taking on the English technical terms for their project.

Although bilingualism had a whole chapter in the English Working Party document (DES and Welsh Office, 1988), the programmes of study for key stage 1 omitted to mention languages other than English in the speaking and listening section. Only Welsh has been singled out for particular mention as being desirable to use in schools. Children will learn best, and learn English best, if they are put in real learning situations, where they need to use language to fulfil their tasks. Teachers should hold on to this, and value all the languages spoken by the children in schools and their importance in the child's learning, whilst, at the same time, helping them to reach the ATs.

Teachers need to organize their own time and classroom space efficiently if the full benefit of group working is to be drawn out. The teacher who sits at a desk trouble-shooting problems with spellings and resources etc, cannot move around to talk with groups and individuals, and that is where good classroom organization is important. A good primary classroom, whether it is a rectangular hut in the playground, or a large airy purpose-built room with areas for play and art and quiet activities, can encourage independence in the children, if properly used. If the resources are well organized and labelled to encourage independent use, and the children are responsible for planning their tasks for the day, they do not have to queue for the teacher to find out what to do next, or where to find equipment. The workshop-based classroom, so common in nursery and infant schools, needs to permeate more junior classes and free the teachers to move around and talk with individuals.

To ensure that the children are being offered a balance of social and curriculum contexts for talk, and to keep track of their progress, good record-keeping is essential, and the ILEA Primary Language Record (ILEA, 1987) has been recommended by the English Working Group (DES and Welsh Office, 1988) as a good model. The matrix on the sampling sheet enables the teacher to record easily, to see at a glance the range of opportunities for talk provided for each child and whether any notes were made at the time. Although record-keeping is time consuming, it is essential to ensure that progress is properly monitored, and effective teaching planned.

A practice in some nursery and reception classes is to keep notebooks hanging in the various areas where the children work. When the teacher and support staff stop in an area and talk with, or observe, the children they can jot notes on particular children in the books and then collect them at the end of the session and transfer the notes to each child's record. It is also only by keeping records that teachers can ensure that *all* the children are being given teacher time and attention. It is easy to overlook some children, especially if they are quiet and do not draw attention to themselves.

## Reading

Recent key texts give substance and backing to what many parents and professionals already know about children – that literacy does not begin at school (Clark, 1976; Clay, 1979; Ferreiro and Teberosky, 1983). There has been substantial research into the effects of environmental print on the growth of children's literacy (Harste, Woodward and Burke, 1984), and there is evidence that some children have learnt to read through the print on television.

A teacher in her first year of teaching in a school in inner London exploited this knowledge and awareness to the full. Sometimes teachers in inner-city areas excuse low reading standards with the claim that the children 'have no experience of books before school', and start with a 'deficit' model of the children, seeing the children as 'the problem'. This often becomes a self-fulfilling prophecy, as shown by Tizard *et al.* (1988). However this teacher started with the knowledge which she knew the children did have. She made a collage of the brand names and logos of products the children were likely to have seen and used – sweets, breakfast cereals and other foods that they were likely to be eating, soap powders and named brands of household goods and labels from local supermarkets. This collage was displayed at children's-eye level in the book corner where the children gathered on entering school in the morning. As the children came in, they pointed to words they knew, such as 'MARS', and 'SAINSBURY'S', and read them with excitement – something familiar, from the world of home, that they could recognize within this strange new world of school. The teacher, joining the group, remarked on what good readers they were, inviting them to display their knowledge:

'Sainsbury's begins with the same as my name.'

'Mars and Mark sound the same.'

The children's knowledge about print was being demonstrated and valued. The children believed in themselves as readers, and could build on this foundation, as the teacher also believed in them. The teacher went on to sort these known words with the children, matching them to an alphabet chart on the wall, creating a new alphabet of environmental print, adding the children's names on the correct initial letter. At the same time, the sharing of good literature was used to extend the children's knowledge and achieve what Marie Clay calls 'talking like a book' (Clay, 1979). As the children became familiar with stories, they made their own versions through shared writing with the teacher, and read other books by the same author. For example, after reading *Mr Gumpy's Outing* by John Burningham, they went on to read *Mr Gumpy's Motor Car*, and made their own version, before a class outing, called 'Class 1's Outing', in which each child asked the teacher if they could come on the outing, and were invited to come 'if they behaved themselves', in the style of the book.

So, in this simple activity, the children were already working towards attainment target 2, level 1:

Pupils should be able to:

* recognise that print is used to carry meaning, in books and in other forms in the everyday world.
* begin to recognise individual words or letters in familiar contexts.
* show signs of a developing interest in reading.
* talk in simple terms about the content of stories, or information in non-fiction books. (DES and Welsh Office, 1989, p. 5)

This is in contrast to the class where all the children embark on the same programme of flash cards bearing the names of the jolly characters in whatever trusty reading scheme is used in the school. This approach creates an aura of strangeness for the child, who quickly learns that this strange thing called 'reading' which s/he has come to school to learn, involves waving bits of card around. When the child has learned to recognize enough words (or even word-bits) s/he may be allowed to take home 'a book' – a slim pamphlet which bears little relationship to her previous experience of books in the home, which are usually thicker and contain meaningful pictures and prose. Literacy is culturally defined (Smith, 1988) and for some children the difference between the literacy of home and the literacy of school is greater than for others. As with speaking and listening, there is a greater likelihood that children will become literate if the literacy they bring to school is recognized, accepted and used as a foundation for growth.

The programme of study for reading clearly states that 'Reading activities should build on the oral language and experiences which children bring from home' (DES and Welsh Office, 1989, p. 15), and this is true for children not only on entering school, but all the way through. Teachers have, as professionals, to work in the first instance with the *children* to discover their previous knowledge and experience, rather than starting with *materials* which dictate the next move.

Having acknowledged the starting points of the children, it is important to be confident about the next step. The introduction of good literature, which will be familiar to many children and an exciting new experience for others, is a crucial early stage (Clark, 1976). The National Curriculum requires the provision of a range of good literature for *all* children. This should be interpreted to mean all children *including* those in the early stages of learning to read, and those for whom reading is not easy. That is, the groups of children who are most likely to be presented with the unnatural and often unsuitable pamphlet-style booklets that form the core of many reading schemes should, under the National Curriculum, be enabled to learn to read with proper books. The important influence of early experience with good books on children's success in learning to read has long been realized (Locke, 1693; Clark, 1976). Now there is an 'official' acknowledgement, through the National Curriculum, that real books make real readers. What is vitally important to note, however, are the skills required of the teacher in fostering reading by this approach.

It is not enough to provide an exciting library and then leave children to learn by themselves, by osmosis; the English Working Group made it clear that children should be developing a range of skills alongside the reading of literature (DES and Welsh Office, 1988). Teachers may need to develop skills to assess and record exactly what children are doing when they read: what concepts of print they have, and what skills they are using.

> As research makes available to us more evidence of the processes of reading and writing and of the ways in which the associations of literacy most powerfully penetrate the operations of our society, ignorance of these processes and functions becomes for teachers both a professional handicap and a shirking of responsibility. (Spencer, 1986)

These are strong words, but the detailed recording of what a child can do as a reader and the planning for further development depend on the teacher having a clear understanding of literacy development in children.

There will be a need for INSET to support staff development in many schools, if children's progress in reading is to be properly monitored. In the report of the English Working Group, it was suggested that the ILEA Primary Language Record 'be adopted as a starting point' for the development of a national system of record-keeping for continuous assessment (DES and Welsh Office, 1988, p. 44). The ILEA Primary Language Record is a good basis for developing profiles of children's language use, starting every year with conferences with the child and parents, and using detailed diagnostic techniques such as miscue analysis for assessing reading behaviour.

The value of working in close partnership with parents to foster literacy in children has long been valued in schools, and the ILEA Primary Language Record enables the parents to help the teacher compile a much more detailed profile of the child as a language user in English and other languages.

However, in ILEA, the Primary Language Record was introduced to schools with an extensive INSET package of its own, involving advisory teacher support, courses for language co-ordinators and whole school staffs, video material and a detailed handbook. It was seen as vital by the team who developed the record that time was taken to develop practice and build the recording and assessment techniques into the fabric of the school's work (ILEA, 1987). The schools adopting the record in the first wave of implementation were those which had identified language as their main focus for development for the year in question. In the rush of development and change across three curriculum areas in the coming year, it is hard to see how the adoption of such a detailed record, however desirable, can be successfully accomplished. The suggestion that continuous assessment should be based on the Primary Language Record is excellent, and offers more hope of assessing attainment than the proposed standard assessment tasks (SATs), but the time scale allowed, with the staff resources available in schools, means that this is probably not workable.

It is explicit in the programmes of study that all children need to have access to good literature and time to read it. Further, all children should be read to by the teacher daily, according to the guidance. This is one of the most welcome suggestions in the National Curriculum and should be interpreted positively. Far too few junior children are read to regularly (Hodgson and Pryke, 1983); reading, when it happens, is too often left to the end of the day when a long novel is brought out which may take a whole term to read piecemeal. The most effective approach is for a range of stories and poems to be read at several times across the day. Short stories, picture books and longer novels should be read aloud. The interest levels of the books should vary, as should the level of textual difficulty, to reflect the range of reading level in the class. Children who are still non-fluent readers benefit from hearing stories at their own level read aloud to extend their repertoire of known books and to facilitate independent reading of the same text later. Also, having the teacher read a book aloud popularizes it and gives it status, and there is less likelihood of a child being stigmatized for reading a book that is 'easier' than those read by others in the class if it is a hot favourite. Competent readers do not read consistently at their highest level of ability. An adult may read a demanding novel, perhaps over several weeks, but read newspapers and magazines in between times, and choose to read the latest blockbuster bestseller in a day. Children, too, need access to a wide range of books and other materials as well as time in school in which to read, if they are to develop as readers and not be content with their simply having achieved literacy.

Where children are in a positive environment for reading, this is reflected in their knowledge of authors and illustrators, their book reviews and their reading journals, which they share and discuss with the teacher during weekly reading conferences. Producing a termly 'Top Ten' author chart is one way of focusing on the reading experiences of the class. Although the class library should provide an exciting choice of books, it should be emphasized that reading does not need to be restricted to books from school. The current book being read may be from the class, school or public library, from the reader's own collection, chosen and bought by him/herself, received as a present, or perhaps borrowed from a friend. There should be provision for and acknowledgement of the *biliteracy* of many children and opportunity should be made for them to read and write in all the languages in which they are literate. Books which have been written and published by the children themselves help to foster an awareness that books are written by authors, and give to their own writing a sense of purpose and a desire for high standards in both composition and transcription.

The programmes of study for English provide clear suggestions for activities rooted in real learning situations across the curriculum and using a range of reading skills with non-fiction books. The suggestion is made that these too could be read aloud to children. The emphasis on continued development of reading ability is welcomed. Here again teachers may need to sharpen their own skills in analysing the reading competence of children, planning for growth without recourse to decontextualized exercises. Children need to be taught how to use non-fiction books properly if they are to avoid the mass copying of chunks from books which often passes for 'project work'. Having a real purpose in using books, perhaps to follow through a first-hand experience, is a good starting point. So, for example, having collected mini-beasts in the school grounds, drawn and observed them, and made notes on what they already know and have found out, children may jot down a few questions before going on to find some appropriate books and using information retrieval skills to find the answers, often incidentally discovering all sorts of other fascinating information.

Time needs to be spent in discussing with children how they found the information from the books and in developing different reading skills. In the early stages of literacy children are often asked to read aloud carefully to the teacher. Therefore, many children later need reassurance that it is 'permissible' to skim through a page if the index has indicated it contains information relevant to their needs. It is even worth encouraging children to include bibliographies to show which books they have found useful and inform others, and this can evolve into an exercise on evaluating the non-fiction books in school.

## Writing

In writing, too, the emphasis should be on noting the child's starting points and then building on them. Children are aware of the print around them and of the adults in their lives who are writing. *All* children experience writing before school, not just those from homes where there has been a definite focus on literacy and a conscious effort to foster it (Hall *et al.*, 1989). The publication of a number of studies of pre-school children's writing, (Ferreiro and Teberosky, 1983; Bissex, 1980; Clay, 1975; Temple, Nathan and Burris, 1982) and the dissemination of good practice based on this knowledge through the National Writing Project's work (SCDC, 1987–9) has led to recognition by teachers that children are entering school with some concepts of print.

Asking groups of teachers to record all the writing they do in 48 hours reveals that much of it is rather mundane and functional such as filling in forms, signing cheques and benefit books, writing shopping lists or the writing connected with running a catalogue. Other forms of writing are linked to work, or for recreation: filling in the pools coupon, word searches, crosswords, recording sports results, cataloguing collections.

Then there are communications such as greetings cards, postcards and letters. Very few children are not involved in these forms of writing from an early age (Hall *et al.*, 1989). But what counts as writing in school may be very different. Children often start in reception classes with teachers who declare that their children 'can't write', when the truth is that the teacher is only judging the child's ability to write or copy a line of prose under a picture.

Where children are in nursery and infant classes with well-provided writing areas, where they can choose to go and write as freely as they can choose to paint or play in the sand, they will write in their own way, at the limits of their levels of understanding and knowledge about print, and reveal their knowledge. If there is a notepad by the phone, children will make notes, and lists for the class shop. If an office is set up, children will write on forms and type, because they know that is what happens in offices. If paper and envelopes and a postbox are there, children will send cards and letters to friends. Children as young as three years old have been able to demonstrate their understanding that drawing and writing are different, and in some cases attempt to write their names (Harste, Woodward and Burke, 1984). The initial stages of writing as represented in level 1 of attainment targets 3, 4 and 5 indicate some of the early writing behaviour of young children. However, one feature was omitted: 'behaving like a writer'. This is where the child may not be trying to convey meaning through the marks on the page, but is exploring *what it is to be a writer* (Czerniewska, 1989), and this is important behaviour to record. The National Writing Project (SCDC, 1987–9) has done much to publicize a developmental approach to writing, focusing on real purposes and contexts for writing. As with the early stages of reading, it is important to begin with the child's own 'writing'. A common teacher-imposed model is to present writing in letters several centimetres high for the child to trace or copy. This approach will not always lead to independent writers producing 'independently, pieces of writing using complex sentences . . .' at level 2 (DES and Welsh Office, 1989). The ATs for writing do seem to be demanding and have caused many anxieties among teachers, who are unsure whether their children will achieve level 3 by the time the SATs arrive. However, we need to examine how far low attainment in writing is affected by low expectations of teachers. The level of expectation in one inner-city school was greatly improved by the work of one nursery teacher.

The teacher set up an inviting writing area where children chose to go and write, using a range of writing implements and formats. She kept dated and annotated samples of the children's writing during the 18–24 months they spent in the nursery, and mounted the work as an exhibition before the children entered the Infants. The very obvious development, from early 'scribbles' to lines of print which were meant to convey a message, was very apparent. The children's obvious interest in writing, in English and other familiar languages, and their levels of understanding about print became apparent to other staff. These teachers then no longer assumed that their new intake 'couldn't write' and were able to work with confident writers and take them further.

Having acknowledged that children are aware of writing across a range of purposes and formats, it is important to offer at least as broad a range of opportunities in school if they are to join the 'literacy club' (Smith, 1988, p. 2) and reach the required ATs. By aiming to develop 'writing through writing', for real purposes, this can more readily be achieved. Too often writing in school is restricted to straight prose accounts describing a visit or an activity which might be better recorded in a different format. What is the purpose of the 'now go and write about it' instruction which so often causes groans from the children? Cooking sessions are an example of this, where there are often no clear aims for the writing. If the writing is to inform others by supplying the recipe for them to follow, then the emphasis should be on accuracy of information and sequencing, although as the children have often been given the printed recipe to follow themselves, it might be more worthwhile to display that. If the aim is to see if the children have remembered the sequence of events, then paper divided into squares for drawings or diagrams with accompanying captions would be an effective record. Photographs with accompanying writing could serve the same purpose and form part of a book recording activities in the classroom, perhaps with a printed text, or one written by the teacher at the children's dictation. The subjective response to the activity, recording the smell of the dough, and what it felt like to mix and knead, could be told and written. If the cooking was part of a scientific investigation, then the findings of different groups might be tabulated. The approach to writing should depend on the nature and aims of the task.

An emphasis on real purposes for writing can lead to publication. This might be either as a wall display or in making books for others to read. This also provides an opportunity for using knowledge about the construction of non-fiction books, with indexes, contents lists, sub-headings. The work will often need to be revised and redrafted, to ensure that what is said is satisfactory, before it is ready for publication and decisions about presentation made. This involves checking for spelling and grammatical accuracy if others are to read the text easily, and deciding whether to write by hand or use mechanical methods of transcription for the final draft.

There has been a welcome return to the teaching of handwriting skills, for developing both fluency and speed in composition and developing calligraphy skills for final presentation. The programmes of study contain suggested progression, but where children's handwriting is at its best in schools, time has been made available for children to practise and explore a range of papers and writing implements, so that informed judgements can be made about the appropriate tools and style for the purpose in hand. Children who only write with 'best' pens for their 'fair copy' may not achieve enough confidence and proficiency with the tools to be confident in their use.

The writing elements of the National Curriculum for English include use of the word-processing facilities on the microcomputer. While any teacher who has used a word processor with children will praise what can be achieved in terms of developing writing and confidence, the practicalities of the situation are complex. In a class of thirty children with one computer, once fixed times for assembly, PE and breaks are removed, and the odd music and swimming lesson subtracted, each child would have at most 30 to 40 minutes a week on the word processor, assuming it was not used for other purposes. Many teachers do not have their own microcomputers, but share with other classes, and the science and maths components of the National Curriculum also have a computer component. These factors drastically reduce the viable time any one child may spend on the word processor. Without a large cash injection to put hardware in schools it will be impossible to deliver this aspect of the National Curriculum properly, whatever the interest and enthusiasm of children and teachers for word processing.

Despite the constraints, teachers have found various ways of coping with the demands on computer time by arriving at compromise solutions and restricting use of the computer for particular writing functions. The word processor might be used for first drafts only, revising and editing from a printout which is then altered on screen for a final draft. Children's first drafts, complete with errors, can be typed in by an adult, leaving the child to use the word processor for editing. The word processor might be used for final drafts only, although a typewriter would be adequate for this. Alternatively, limited computer time might be concentrated on particular groups of children who would gain most benefit. For example, a concept keyboard can be used to help children build confidence in the early stages of composition, either by having key words related to a topic or model of writing or by having individual sheets for each child with the words s/he wants to use. It might also be considered useful to give priority on the word processor to children who have difficulties with writing, since it frees the children who have poor motor control in writing. Those with spelling problems find it less emotive to correct words on screen than to change or rewrite in a book, where it often makes the writing look a mess.

The distinction between the composition and transcription aspects of writing has been highlighted in the ATs and this is most welcome even at the earliest stages of children's writing. Where children are confident in their writing, and feel free to take risks with spelling new words themselves rather than rely on the few words in their sight vocabularies, the quality of the writing is often much better. What is important, though, is that children are taught how to learn spellings when the need arises. Spelling ability depends on visual awareness, and as adults we often write a word to see if it looks right to check it before resorting to a dictionary. Children who have not been taught how to *learn* how to spell tend to recite the letters in sequence and learn them as a string, which is not helpful (see Chapter 2). Where word books are used to collect some unknown words, they should be dynamic learning tools, rather than static word collections, and children can be encouraged to learn by the LOOK, COVER, WRITE, CHECK method in spare moments or timetabled sessions. Spelling errors commonly involve the transposition of some remembered letters, or the misapplication of a phonic rule, and the errors can be learning points. If children are encouraged, when they have misspelt a word, to compare it with the real spelling and to check first which parts of the word they got right, before focusing on the part causing problems, they develop a more positive view of themselves as spellers.

A great disappointment in the orders for key stage 1 has been the inclusion in the programme of study of the following passage: 'They should be taught, in the context of discussion about their own writing, grammatical terms such as sentence, verb, tense, noun, pronoun' (DES and Welsh Office, 1989, p. 18).

Some terminology is essential for children to be able to talk about what they are doing; for example knowing the difference between a word and a letter, in making explicit the knowledge implicit in children's command of spoken and written English, will develop children's metalinguistic awareness of language. But it is necessary to question the inclusion of such prescriptive knowledge about language in key stage 1, when both the English Working Group (DES and Welsh Office, 1988) and the National Curriculum Council (NCC, 1989) were clearly not in favour of such early blanket introduction of grammatical terms. It is possible to discuss with a child the absence of a verb in a sentence by demonstrating that it does not sound right, without actually calling the missing part a verb. The usual description of verb is a 'doing' word. So ask any class of infants to pick out the verb in this sentence, 'My sister is a swimmer', and it is likely they would pick out the noun, 'swimmer'. Defining parts of speech is not as easy as it seems!

As professionals, teachers must monitor aspects of the National Curriculum, and if they feel these are unworkable, fight for their modification. The most effective way to evaluate writing across a wide range of purposes and styles is through continuous assessment. A test cannot synthesize the same breadth of experience and assess children's competence in depth. If efficient methods of assessing the children's writing development are in place before the arrival of the first SATs, it may be possible to highlight the relative inefficiency of the test procedures. The National Writing Project materials (SCDC, 1987–9) and the ILEA Primary Language Record (ILEA, 1987), combined with the record-keeping practices already being explored in other LEAs have proved extremely helpful in informing teachers about children's writing development.

## CONCLUSION

The key factors in implementing the National Curriculum then, are to review current practice, reject obsolete practices, and plan for staff development where necessary. There is also a need to review the National Curriculum itself, feeding back data and experiences from schools to ensure that it becomes a useful framework for educational planning. While having sympathy with the concerns and despair of people such as Michael Rosen (1989) about a narrowing of the curriculum and the horrors of testing, those in teaching are in a position to affect the development of the National Curriculum, as suggested in Chapter 1. It is important that the documents produced for English from 1988 to 1990 are not regarded as complete, but continue to reflect good practice in language as it develops in schools. There is still the possibility of shaping the National Curriculum into a useful set of guidelines for teachers so that they can plan for and evaluate their children's learning effectively.

## REFERENCES

Barnes, D., Britton, J. and Rosen, H. (1971) *Language, the Learner and the School*. Harmondsworth: Penguin Books.
Bernstein, B. (1971) *Class, Codes and Control*. London: Routledge and Kegan Paul.
Bissex, G. (1980) *Gnys at Work: a Child Learns to Read and Write*. Cambridge, MA: Harvard University Press.

Britton, J. (1970) *Language and Learning.* Harmondsworth: Penguin Books.

*Child Education* (1989) Leamington Spa: Scholastic Publications (June).

Clark, M. (1976) *Young Fluent Readers.* London: Heinemann.

Clay, M. (1975) *What Did I Write?* London: Heinemann.

Clay, M. (1979) *The Early Detection of Reading Difficulties.* London: Heinemann.

Czerniewska, P. (1989) Finding the right words. *Times Educational Supplement*, 17 March.

DES (1975) *A Language for Life* (The Bullock Report). London: HMSO.

DES (1988) *Report of Committee of Inquiry into the Teaching of the English Language.* London: HMSO.

DES and Welsh Office (1988) *English for Ages 5 to 11.* London: DES and Welsh Office.

DES and Welsh Office (1989) *English in the National Curriculum.* London: HMSO.

Ferreiro, E. and Teberosky, A. (1983) *Literacy before Schooling.* London: Heinemann.

Flanders, N. (1970) *Analysing Teacher Behaviour.* Reading, MA: Addison-Wesley.

Galton, M., Simon, B., and Croll, P. (1980) *Inside the Primary Classroom.* London: Routledge and Kegan Paul.

Graves, D. (1983) *Writing: Teachers and Children at Work.* London: Heinemann.

Hall, N. *et al.* (1989) *Parents' Views on Writing and the Teaching of Writing.* Manchester: Department of Education Studies, Manchester Polytechnic (for the National Writing Project).

Halliday, M. A. K. (1978) *Language as Social Semiotic.* London: Edward Arnold.

Harste, J., Woodward, V. A., and Burke, C. L. (1984) *Language Stories and Literacy Lessons.* Portsmouth: Heinemann.

Heath, S. B. (1983) *Ways with Words.* Cambridge: Cambridge University Press.

Hodgson, J. and Pryke, D. (1983) *Reading: Competence at 6 and 10.* Shrewsbury: Shropshire LEA.

ILEA (1987) *The Primary Language Record: Handbook for Teachers* London: Centre for Language in Primary Education, ILEA.

ILEA Schools Psychological Service Journal *Gnosis* (now distributed by LDA, Duke St., Wisbech, Cambs.).

Locke, J. (1922) *Educational Writings.* Cambridge: Cambridge University Press.

NCC (1989) *National Curriculum Council Consultation Report: English 5 to 11.* York: NCC.

National Oracy Project (1989) *Talk.* York: NCC.

Richmond, J. (1986) Teachers of writing need a clearer view. In National Writing Project (1986) *Talk.* London: SCDC.

Rosen, M. (1989) But me no buts. *Times Educational Supplement*, 12 May.

SCDC (School Curriculum Development Committee) (1987–9) *About Writing*. London: SCDC.

Smith, F. (1988) *Joining the Literacy Club*. London: Heinemann.

Spencer, M. (1986) Emergent literacies: A site for analysis. *Language Arts* 63 (5) September. 443–453.

Temple, C. A., Nathan, R. G. and Burris, N. A. (1982) *The Beginnings of Writing*. Boston: Allyn and Bacon.

Tizard, B., and Hughes, M. (1984) *Young Children Learning*. London: Fontana.

Tizard, B., Blatchford, P., Burke, J., Farquhar, C. and Plewis, I. (1988) *Young Children at School in the Inner City*. London: Lawrence Erlbaum

Townsend, J. R. (1965) *Written for Children*. Cambridge: Cambridge University Press.

Wells, C. G. (1986) *The Meaning Makers*. London: Heinemann.

# Chapter 7

# Implementing the National Curriculum for Mathematics

*David Clemson*

This chapter suggests a strategy which will implement the National Curriculum statutory orders and also preserve and foster good primary practice. It is structured to inform planning at relevant stages:

Stage 1 – formulating a school policy.
Stage 2 – school policy implementation.
Stage 3 – planning programmes of study.

Though reference will be made to statutory requirements the discussion will broaden to address current educational issues which are essential factors for developing a positive mathematics programme.

## INTRODUCTION

From autumn 1989 state schools have the legal responsibility to provide a mathematics programme which develops appropriate and transferable skills through realistic contextual settings. The Attainment Targets (ATs) define actual content and detail relevant skills for specific age phases, while the non-statutory guidance (NSG) assists planning for progression and continuity, and recommends effective teaching and learning strategies. *All* children now have the legal entitlement to a mathematics programme which develops confidence, competence and the ability to cope in 'real' problem situations. As a consequence, a successful primary mathematics programme will be one which effectively develops mathematical concepts and utilizes everyday experiences within the classroom environment to introduce and practise essential skills.

A perennial problem with school mathematics is that a large proportion of curriculum time is spent practising what is already known. To avoid notions of content inaccessibility there is the need for an ongoing element of exploration and imaginative play. Teachers should be offering tasks which involve ownership and freedom in choosing both strategy and communication of outcome. Through the medium of investigation there is opportunity to explore within mathematics itself, utilizing imagination, probing concepts and testing personal frameworks, no matter how elementary. The National Curriculum imaginatively delivered will provide all this as a minimum entitlement; for the talented few who have a gift for the abstract elements of pure mathematics, a specialist syllabus will be provided at the appropriate point. School mathematics would therefore be concerned with both developing useful life skills and building positive attitudes towards the subject. A feeling would be engendered that proficiency is a personal measure rather than a comparison with the class norm. An individual will have the right to expect mathematical experiences which allow success while using personal competencies, at whatever level.

The aim of mathematics education will be to develop a confident, autonomous mathematician: a flexible thinker, who will endeavour to seek a solution, devise a solving strategy and utilize appropriate skills from a well-established personal repertoire. In the past too many children have left school with a pot-pourri of shaky skills and disembodied algorithms which have proved to have little practical application. Far too many mechanical skills and abstract algorithms are being learned 'by heart' for no apparent practical application and certainly without essential underlying conceptual understanding. Interesting though they may be for a minority of children, should simultaneous and quadratic equations, for instance, form a compulsory part of the mathematics diet for *all* secondary-aged children? 'If a skill has no obvious everyday application then perhaps time should not be spent developing it' (DES and Welsh Office, 1982, Para. 267).

Teachers should be aware that competence in mathematics is not merely manipulation of numbers but also about communication techniques; ways of viewing and making sense of the environment, about ability with confidence to solve realistic and everyday problems utilizing a well-established and understood repertoire of transferable skills. Though the competent use of mechanical skills is important in working towards this end, it should never be considered an end in its own right. Children should be able instantly and accurately to recall basic facts, addition and subtraction bonds to 99, multiplication facts to 10 × 10. After this minimum mental requirement is established practical problems should introduce and consolidate subsequent skills and processes. Skills are resources to be used and, as such, they must be in a usable form.

The Cockcroft Committee was set up in 1978 to examine why schools were not able to deliver the necessary skills and competencies required for industry and commerce. In essence the findings were critical of much of secondary mathematics and of the negative attitude most children had developed during their school experience towards the subject.

> Mathematics lessons in secondary schools are very often not about anything. You collect like terms, or learn the laws of indices, with no perception of why anyone needs to do such things There is excessive preoccupation with sequence of skills and quite inadequate opportunity to see the skills emerging from the solution of problems. (DES and Welsh Office, 1982, Para. 462)

In support of these findings and with the intention of assisting teachers in curriculum improvement, *Mathematics from 5 to 16* (DES and Welsh Office, 1985) was produced. Particularly prescriptive in its recommendations, it boldly stated that the aim of school mathematics is ultimately to develop the autonomous mathematician. Principal qualities of an autonomous mathematician are that he or she: has persistence and perseverance; is aware a solution must exist; remains dedicated until personally satisfied with an outcome; has confidence in her/his ability to communicate and express mathematical ideas through a variety of media; displays competence in relevant basic and mental skills; shows ability to determine and apply appropriate skills; exhibits a flexible and imaginative use of skills; utilizes a variety of calculating aids efficiently and effectively. Within this profile, competence in mechanical skills is to be viewed in relative terms. Though essential to the complete mathematician these skills account for one-sixth of the complete profile. Skills are 'tools' to work with, and do not usefully exist out of context, they are useful only in solving problems.

The NSG offers considerable support in this endeavour and suggests that the statutory orders should be imaginatively implemented towards similar goals. 'Mathematics is a set of inter-related ideas; it is not made up of separate elements which can be taught in isolation from one another' (NCC, 1989a, Para. 5.2).

> Learning skills, such as adding two numbers, calculating the area of a triangle or solving an equation, form a large part of the pupil's work in school mathematics. Important though they are, such skills are only a means to an end, and should be taught and learned in a context that provides a meaning. (NCC, 1989a, Para. 2.4)

Though several advisory documents and papers have been written in the past recommending similar 'missions', they were not backed by statutory orders. For the first time the purpose of teaching mathematics has been legally established and widely publicized. Though the precedent set could be sinister, in the instance of mathematics there is nothing for teachers to fear from the National Curriculum proposals and much for pupils to gain. No longer should parents accept their reception class children doing pages of sums or other inappropriate tasks. Nor should secondary-aged children suffer mathematical myopia reinforced through discrete subject boundaries in neat timetabled slots. Teachers will have time and support to concentrate on developing relevant concepts rather than hastily building unstable skills. Though the content has been explicitly described, decisions about pedagogy, context, organization and implementation are still very much the province of teachers with knowledge of their children. There is some hope that National Curriculum content, set within imaginative programme of study in the context of good primary practice, will succeed in raising standards. More importantly, it offers schools another opportunity fully to develop child autonomy. The effective implementation of a National

Curriculum will require a critical analysis of all aspects of school mathematics education as it exists at present.


## FORMULATING A SCHOOL POLICY

This section covers the next stage of effective implementation: the formulation of a school policy. A policy statement explicitly describes the role of mathematics education within the specific school setting. The policy will form a negotiated statement unambiguously defining curriculum aims and learning objectives with direct reference to the individual school and its community. The writing team should ideally comprise headteacher, representatives of the staff, governors and parents, representation from the LEA and the local community. Content would be informed by statutory orders, NSG, LEA guidelines, recent and relevant reports. Relevant papers will not only be those specific to mathematics but all those concerned with the primary curriculum.

The school working party should achieve consensus in their recommendations and the resulting document should be unambiguous in particular key areas: aims of teaching mathematics; statements on permeation issues; recommended teaching strategies and effective curriculum delivery; agreed criteria for organization – school, age phase, classes and groups; learning objectives; cross-curricular implications; assessment criteria; record-keeping; effective use of resources and equipment; arrangements for involving parents.

While involved in constructing a policy statement for any subject area it is essential that the working group is fully aware of current educational issues. With a more complete understanding of such issues, responsive and sensitive schemes of work will be designed and programmes of study implemented which offer all children the opportunity to achieve their full potential. As this chapter endeavours to assist effective implementation of the National Curriculum it is necessary to address contemporary issues, particularly those relevant to mathematics education.

British society is multicultural. Children need to have a clear understanding that society is composed of contrasting but equivalent cultures. Mathematics offers schools the opportunity to raise an awareness of how other cultures have influenced the development of mathematics to its present state.

It is possible to make positive use of mathematical ideas drawn from other cultures, especially when discussing shape and space. For example many of the Rangoli patterns which are used by Hindu and Sikh families to decorate their homes on important occasions have a geometrical basis in which symmetry plays a major part . . . As children grow older, it is possible to discuss the ways in which the numerals which we use have developed from those which were originally used in eastern countries, and the contribution to the development of mathematics which have come from different countries and different cultures. (DES and Welsh Office, 1982, Para. 224)

It is crucially important that *all* children are aware of the cultural origins of mathematics and its influence upon the evolution of the discipline. Mathematics in its present accepted form owes much to a non-European heritage. The number and function symbols themselves are an adaptation from the Hindu-Arabic systems. Recording time in sets of 60 is from Babylonia. Terms, units and formulae for calculating area were established by ancient Egyptians and computer technology owes its existence to algebra (Mohammed ibn musa al-Khowarizmi), established AD 820. It is from this rich heritage that mathematics has been able to develop today's technologies. Appliances that are taken for granted as part of our everyday western existence have an ancestry outside Europe. It is possible, even at an early age, to enrich children's understanding and raise cultural awareness by reference to number systems and mathematical application around the world.

Recently several researchers have looked into records of attainment in mathematics and particularly the discrepancy between the achievement of boys and girls (Burton, 1986). From data gathered, particularly from secondary schools, it is clear that a significant proportion of the school population is underachieving. This appears principally as the result of teacher attitude, use of stereotypical images in pupils' materials and parental expectations (Burton, 1986). Teachers are often unaware of the enormous effect they have upon building attitudes and reinforcing stereotypes (Centre for Mathematics Education, 1986). Although the obvious signs of underachievement and negativity materialize in the secondary school, attitudes are established at a much younger age. It is not uncommon to witness examples of gender bias and sexual discrimination within nursery and reception classes. If girls are to have opportunity in achieving their full potential in mathematics then teachers must consciously offer equality and positive reinforcement to all members of the class regardless of gender. Teachers should be aware of the effect, and sensitive in the choice, of the context within which mathematics is developed. Girls must feel that mathematics is applicable and accessible. Teachers need to pay much more attention to the way group work is organized particularly when practical apparatus and workshops are involved. An essential element of investigational mathematics and problem-solving is taking responsibility for your own actions and justifying those decisions when challenged. It is important that all members of the class are given support to develop confidence and take considered risks. Initially girls will need support and encouragemet to take part in group discussions fully, particularly when personal solving strategies are being defended. There should be no difference in what teachers expect from any sub-group in the class. Much pupil material perpetuates sexual stereotyping. For instance, care should be taken that work-card illustrations do not show boys actively involved in practical measuring while a girl records the results. It is important that teachers are not only aware of the power of such images but proactive in refusing to use them within their classes. It is crucial that school policies both recommend positive action and monitor implementation in the two important areas of multicultural education and non-sexist mathematics.

Information technology is now an integral part of the primary school curriculum. The National Curriculum, as a whole, describes specific tasks which should be carried out using a computer. Mathematics ATs 11, 12, 13 and 14 detail experiences which cannot successfully be introduced or consolidated without children having prolonged access to computers. *Curriculum Matters: Information Technology from 5 to 16* (DES, 1989a), the *Report on Information Technology in Initial Teacher Training* (DES, 1989b) and *Technology in the National Curriculum* (DES and Welsh Office, 1990) are all of one opinion. Within mathematics, English, science and design and technology quite dramatic changes are called for in curriculum content and assessment of outcomes.

> These initiatives can only hasten the development of a situation where the use of IT [information technology] becomes a normal part of everyday learning for the majority of pupils. In addition to establishing strategies for the permeation of IT through all areas of the curriculum, many LEAs' policies for IT in schools already set down a range of specific IT experiences which all pupils are expected to have had by particular stages in their school career. (DES, 1989b, Para. 9)

Teachers now have a legal obligation to offer children IT experiences both as an essential component in the learning process of all subjects and also as a set of discrete and powerful lifeskills.

Primary teachers are well aware of the need to start teaching from where the child is. In the past, primary schools have had little outside pressure to achieve predetermined targets. The progression through the curriculum and speed of learning were dictated very much by the child's performance and the experience of the teacher. A child's performance was recorded mainly for diagnostic purposes to inform teachers of educational needs and to assist in planning personal programmes of study. The element of the National Curriculum legislation which has raised most criticism is the proposal to implement a standardized assessment procedure. Children working within legislated curriculum content would be assessed on their progress at four key stages: 7, 11, 14 and 16 years. The results of these tests would be reported externally. Within the proposed assessment procedure there appears to lie at least one major difficulty. Within a standardized assessment procedure the group norm determines the success or failure of the individual. As a driving school could efficiently be assessed by the number of test passes then schools could be excused for assessing internal success by the number of passes at key stages. If this becomes an important indicator of attainment then teachers might be justified in teaching to the test. The importance of the individual could be forfeit for the sake of the school profile. Such a situation would be in direct opposition to good primary practice. The assessment of the individual should inform decisions on content and strategies for future development for the individual. It is essential that teachers regard the National Curriculum as an aid in devising personal development programmes. The child should not be made to fit the National Curriculum, rather the curriculum should be designed to meet the needs of the individual. Though teachers have always kept records for the class and individual there is now a need for standardization, across subject, school and country. For full compatibility of format and terminology, teachers will now refer to National Curriculum guidelines for all core subject areas. As assessment procedures are established, the levels of attainments and bench-mark tests will analyse each child's progress, allowing teachers a complete and accurate profile to inform future action. National assessment machinery will be in place by 1991 through standard assessment tasks (SATs). For key stage I there are indications that these will partly be based upon teachers' records and in-school assessment procedures. It should not be assumed that national assessment procedures will invariably comprise formal, subject-specific tests, though see Chapter 1 on the role of testing. There is no urgency for schools to devise and complete comprehensive record sheets at the moment. 'All that needs to be recorded in the first year are the experiences the child has done' (Gabriel Goldstein, IT in the Information Technology in Teacher Education National Conference, 1989). To support national test results, staff need to devise cross-curricular assessment tasks which allow children freedom to demonstrate what they can do in realistic and culturally applicable contexts. They need to provide an assessment environment which offers a child the scope and opportunity to utilize personal skills in appropriate and meaningful situations.

An example of a cross-curricular assessment task for mathematics, key stage 2, might focus on designing a space-efficient bedroom. While tackling the project a child would have to plan a course of action, use interdependent skills from separate subjects areas and to make decisions about how the outcomes could best be communicated to an audience (see Figure 7.1).

Mathematics is a process concerned with solving real-life problems. The aim of school mathematics must therefore be concerned with developing competence in using a range of transferable skills. To introduce and consolidate these skills it is essential that they are framed within realistic situations and consolidated through practical workshops. Headteachers should be fully aware of the resource implications involved in implementing the statu-

*Subject-specific activities*:

| | |
|---|---|
| Mathematics | Measurement, modelling (3D & 2D), use of scale, plans, nets, costing, materials, representing outcomes. |
| Science | What is needed in a bedroom: essential, preferred, luxury? What is acceptable space? |
| Design & Technology | Designing beds with cupboards and drawers, folddown desks, multipurpose lighting. |

**Figure 7.1** Design a space-efficient bedroom

tory orders in a manner recommended by the NSG, and teachers should receive support to introduce alternative teaching strategies to cope with limited resources and to develop confidence in newer areas of prescribed content. Staff should not be expected to learn on the job, particularly in newer areas of mathematics and non-traditional modes of teaching. For example, AT11 requires adequate access to computers, turtles and an appropriate workspace. Providing these for all children might present serious problems for some schools. AT11 also specifically states than an understanding of shape and space should be facilitated through experiences in elementary motion geometry and Logo. AT12, 13 and 14 are concerned with data handling and are essentially computer specific. AT1 and 9 are concerned with 'using and applying mathematics' – utilizing multiple skills to solve open-ended problems in realistic cultural contexts. Staff will need to develop resource banks of suitable topics while individual teachers will require time and support to develop confidence and competence in less traditional aspects of mathematics.

To work out number problems most adults do not use the method they were taught in school. It seems that people develop their own methods and procedures to arrive at a solution. Though these methods are varied and diverse, each is equally correct and acceptable, as long as it is effective over multiple instances. Such alternative methods have been personally constructed and are therefore extremely robust in that people remember them and can apply them to a range of problems. As teachers we should be encouraging children to tackle a number problem using five different methods rather than present them with five different sums to be done in the same way. Children should be given experience using a variety of algorithms generated from alternative conceptual models, and freedom and support to create and validate their own casual methods.

> Some low attaining pupils have great difficulty in carrying out and recording computation using standard routines. However, after discussion and practical work with appropriate counting materials, they are often able to carry out calculations successfully by making use of methods of their own devising. (DES and Welsh Office, 1982, Para. 267)

Mathematics provides a powerful means of communication. It is a process by which we make sense of our environment. Though they are an essential part of mathematical competence, mechanical skills are merely the tools to assist the exploration. As a process mathematics has outcomes. To be of any value, solutions must be recorded in an appropriate manner and outcomes communicated to an audience. The choice and style of presentation will depend largely upon the context of the problem/investigation and the desired audience response. Children of all ages should have experience in communicating mathematics for a purpose to a stated audience. AT13 is specifically concerned with representing data in a variety of styles for particular purposes. Cross-curricular topics offer the medium for children to utilize a wide variety of communication techniques to inform an audience of work undertaken and outcomes. It is unfortunate if mathematics is recorded only as 'sums' on paper. Much better if solutions are illustrated and illuminated through a variety of representational vehicles (see Figure 7.2).

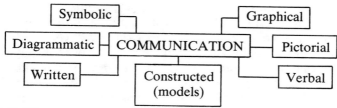

**Figure 7.2**

## IMPLEMENTATION OF SCHOOL POLICY

If the broad outlines contained in the school policy statement are to influence practice it is necessary to produce a 'scheme of work'. This document outlines the delivery of the policy statement to the children in the classrooms. From autumn 1989 this essentially refers to a legal responsibility for schools to teach the statutory orders. The responsibility for developing, and overall custody of, a scheme is that of a headteacher, who is accountable to the governors in the first instance and then to the LEA. The writing of schemes is usually done through staff working parties in consultation with appropriate external agencies. Though the format should not be prescribed, some examples of the content of a model statement are provided here.

A stimulating classroom is one which motivates child enquiry, develops interests and supports notions of ownership. As an aspect of the primary experience, mathematics should be promoted as vibrant and exciting. In practice developing a stimulating environment can be achieved relatively easily. Schools are currently aware of the importance of display for most curriculum areas. Some elements of mathematics within cross-curricular topics are already being effectively displayed, for example pictorial representations, graphs, tables and charts. Teachers should consider the outcomes of mathematical investigations, constructions, puzzles or games as providing material for 2D and 3D display. As previously mentioned, a crucial aspect of mathematical competence is an ability to communicate mathematics. Children having responsibility for display could offer opportunities for decision-making, sharing and informing. Worktop collections can be made of natural objects for 'hands-on' experience of counting, sorting, classification, seriation by a variety of attributes and a mathematical interest table comprising a weekly puzzle of investigation. These can be prepared by children for children. A school mathematics magazine for children and parents could be published termly to contain puzzles, investigations, games and competitions, and examples of children's work. This could be produced within the classroom using IT, by children for children and parents. Displays of mathematical applications such as models, routes, maps and decision charts from adventure games, and number patterns could easily be organized. A study of symmetry and tessellation would offer much material for an effective and colourful display. A stimulating classroom environment would allow open access to new technology. Computers can be used for graph building, word processing, spreadsheets, adventure games, Logo and calculators. Parents appear to be an underused resource in many classrooms. They can assist teachers by constructing and conducting mathematical games. Children should be involved in the decision-making as much as possible; the classroom environment should be the teacher's and the children's joint responsibility. Likewise criteria for display should based upon individual effort and personal achievement and not be dictated by the products of the high achievers.

The Cockcroft Report, although also not wishing to indicate a definitive style for teaching of mathematics, was prepared to provide a list of essential opportunities mathematics teaching should include:

Exposition by the teacher;
Discussion between teacher and pupils and between pupils themselves;
Appropriate practical work;
Consolidation and practice of fundamental skills and routines;
Problem solving, including the application of mathematics to everyday situations;
Investigational work. (DES and Welsh Office, 1982, Para. 243)

Although not explicit in defining teaching styles, there is no doubt this suggests alternatives from the traditional rows-of-desks delivery of class lessons. Children are to be given opportunities to learn independently and collaboratively. To achieve this, teachers should adopt teaching strategies which allow the children freedom, and still give appropriate support to develop self-confidence. For children to become autonomous they must be given opportunity and support in making decisions. If children are provided opportunities and time to think things through and a forum to present personal arguments then teachers are helping to develop self-sufficiency. The learning environment itself should stimulate and question rather than contain and answer. Displays should involve interaction through questioning as well as being informative and stimulating. Children should have feelings of ownership in the classroom, of its resources and the learning process. When a child owns something it becomes personal and crucially important. Teachers should strive to promote the classroom as belonging to all members of the class and not as an alien environment. This involves bringing children's culture and community into the learning environment and reflecting life as the children know it. The child's role in the classroom should be as an equal partner with the teacher. Together they would be involved in making decisions which affect themselves and others.

It is important that a child understands thoroughly the concept involved and can effectively transfer the associated skill to appropriate and alternative situations. The teacher's role in this is to take full advantage of the child's natural curiosity and develop an inquisitive and adaptable thinker. For much of the mathematics curriculum this involves becoming a fellow traveller rather than a leader: someone who supports children to formulate their own understandings by providing alternative models. An interactive classroom provides opportunity for open questioning support in taking risks and an overall atmosphere of security. In a technological society skills previously accepted as essential like log tables and long multiplication soon become redundant; teachers should be aware that skills commonly regarded as indispensable today may well be obsolete in ten years time. Though the curriculum content is prescribed through statutory orders, fostering understanding, pedagogy and developing attitudes are still very much the responsibility of the teacher. There is no reason to suppose that the good practice cited earlier cannot exist within an imposed framework. There are two years to cover the contents of key stage 1 and a further four years working towards stage 2.

In view of the reduced content there is ample time effectively to develop confidence and competence in mathematics.

## PLANNING PROGRAMMES OF STUDY

Throughout this chapter the intention has been to help to implement the National Curriculum in a manner which will develop positive school policies, to devise effective schemes of work and to describe planning programmes of study. As implementation converges towards the classroom so the responsibility shifts from outside agencies through staff custody and finally to teacher guardianship. The success of the National Curriculum lies with the classroom teachers and not the policy-makers in Westminster.

Schemes of work themselves would not contain topic outlines or definitive lesson plans; these are still the province of individual teachers who are aware of content to be covered and have knowledge of the competencies and previous experiences of their classes. At the initial planning stage it is suggested that teachers should *not* look to the ATs and devise programmes of study which attempt to embrace all mathematics attainment targets (NCC, 1989a). They should select a topic and construct an opportunities web diagram as is current practice, illustrating activities and experiences that could be generated from a topic/theme. Then, and only then, should the topic web be compared to attainment profiles to see how the planned activities cover the breadth of mathematical experience. A simple record sheet would record the attainment targets covered and which levels that particular activity/experience might support. It is likely that some attainment targets will be covered several times within a topic while others will have no obvious link. This is desirable, as the transferability of a skill from one situation to another supports the notion of skills as tools, thus consolidating the concept rather than merely the mechanical process.

Should topic planning describe an element of mathematics which has no obvious reference in the statutory orders then fundamental questions would need to be asked. Is the activity essential to the child's mathematical development? If the activity can be justified then it should be included. If it cannot legitimately be defended then children's time need not be wasted. In this way the National Curriculum can act as a valuable arbiter. An activity can provide learning opportunities at different levels, at the same time assisting in matching ability to task. For example, the following sample topic provides opportunity to develop competence in AT12 at four levels, sorting by attribute (level 1) to the creation and interrogation of a computer database (level 4). Effective planning should provide learning opportunities which develop cross-discipline skills at several levels and not merely catalogue isolated activities rehearsing discrete attainment targets at specific levels. Rather than contrive links, areas of mathematical experience not present could be provided for during subsequent topics. Within the two years for key stage 1 and an additional four years to key stage 2, there should be ample opportunity to consolidate skills and develop concepts through a variety of themes, topics and applicable contexts.

## SAMPLE TOPIC 1 – READY TEDDY GO!

*Age range:* Middle infants.
*Duration:* 6 weeks (half term).
*Equipment:* Class collection of teddy bears.
*Organization:* Groups in non-directed workshop.
*Aims:* Developing the autonomous mathematician.
*Summary:* Essential aspects of early mathematics will be introduced and consolidated through the theme of teddy bears. Each member of the class will be asked to loan their bear for the duration of the topic. The teacher will then have available a collection of known items from which a wide variety of mathematical activities can be generated. Each aspect will be explained briefly, followed by an example task.

A. *Sorting* by a variety of attributes, e.g. fur colour, age, sex.

   Task –   Which fur-colour set has the most members?

B. *Seriation* by variety of attributes, e.g. height, waist, weight.

   Task –   Put the bears in order by height.

C. *Measurement* using arbitrary units; make comparisons and use appropriate language.

   Task –   Which bear is the tallest?

D. *Data collection* investigating individual differences to develop binary decision trees using 'Branch' or 'Sorting Game' software.

Task –    In which ways are the bears the same, and in which ways are they different?

E. *Data storage* creating and interrogating a simple database using 'Ourfacts' software.

Task –    Which bear has blue eyes and pink fur?

F. *Data presentation* creating simple block graphs of attributes, e.g. height, weight, waist size, fur colour.

Task –    Build a chart to show the different fur colours in our set.

G. *Counting skills* making sashes with number/word symbols for each bear.

Task –    Can you put the bears back into number order?

H. *Counting skills* using traditional and child/teacher-created counting songs.

Task –    Point to the bear/number in the song.

I. *Teddy stories* using simple sequencing, chronology.

Task –    Retell the story using your own words and pictures.

J. *Information Technology* text/image processing.

Task –    Make a mathematical story book about our bears.

K. *Computation* creating simple board games around theme to consolidate counting skills and number bonds.

Task –    Design and build a simple board game.

L. *One to one correspondence* using 'Goldilocks and the Three Bears' as the context for practical mathematical activities.

Task –    Are there enough spoons, beds, bowls for each bear?

M. *Spatial awareness* using 'Goldilocks and the Three Bears' as the context for developing an understanding of immediate positional terms, e.g. up, down, under, over, above, below.

Task –    Describe where items/characters are in relation to others.

N. *Spatial awareness* using *Winnie the Pooh* as the context for developing use of directional terms: right, left, forward, backward, up, down.

Task – Describe and record Piglet's journey to Pooh's house.

O. *Spatial awareness* using *Winnie the Pooh* as the setting for developing an understanding of locational terms, e.g. under the table, on the chair, near the stairs.

Task – Hide a honey pot in Pooh's house and give clues for another child to find it.

P. *Problem-solving* using *Winnie the Pooh* story to generate problems requiring elementary design technology.

Task – Pooh is stuck in Rabbit's doorway. Can you design and build a machine to get him out?

Q. *Problem-solving* Multiple-skill project.

Task – Plan a picnic for five bears.

R. *Shape* experimenting with and investigating properties of shape to provide opportunities for design and technology.

Task – Plan and make a chair, bed, house, car, shirt for your bear.

S. *Motion geometry* introducing, developing and consolidating spatial awareness within a Logo environment. Build a seat on Turtle's back, and a garage.

Task – Tell turtle to carry teddy home.

T. *Mathematical language*. Throughout the topic take every opportunity to encourage and support the use of correct mathematical language and terminology.

Task – Keep a record of all the mathematical words used during this topic.

At this point teachers could complete a simple scope chart which compares the planned activities with the prescribed content of the statutory orders, recording which ATs are evident at which levels the activity could support.

Topic: Ready Teddy Go!          Age: Middle Infant

| Questions, tasks | Attainment targets | Support levels |
|---|---|---|
| H, I, K, Q, T | AT1 Using and Applying ATs 1–8 | 1, 2 |
| G, H, K, T | AT2 Number and Number notation | 1, 2 |
| G, H, K, T | AT3 Number operations | 1, 2, 3 |
| C, D, E, T | AT4 Estimate and Approximate number | 1, 2 |
| L, H, F, T | AT5 Patterns, relationships and sequences | 1, 2 |
|  | AT6 Functions, formulae, equations and inequalities |  |
|  | AT7 Graphical representation of algebraic functions |  |
| B, C, D, T | AT8 Appreciate nature of measurement | 1, 2 |
| A, D, E, F, P, S, T | AT9 Shape and space and handle data in practical tasks | 1, 2 |
| R, S, T | AT10 Shape and space—2D and 3D | 1, 2 |
| M, N, O, S, T | AT11 Location and transformation in the study of space | 1, 2 |
| A, D, E, T | AT12 Collect, record and process data | 1, 2, 3 |
| F, J, T | AT13 Represent and interpret data | 1, 2, 3 |
|  | AT 14 Understand, estimate and calculate probabilities |  |

## SAMPLE TOPIC 2 – MATHEMATICAL SMARTIES

*Age range:* Top Juniors.
*Duration:* 6 weeks (half term).
*Equipment:* Sufficient tubes of 'Smarties' for practical activities.
*Organization:* Groups in non-directed workshop.
*Aims:* Developing the autonomous mathematician.
*Instructions:* Use the following questions as a starting point for your investigations. Present your findings to the rest of the class in an effective and interesting manner.

(a) Are there always the same number of sweets in each tube?

(b) Is a tube the best package to hold these sweets?

(c) Which colour is most popular in our school?

(d) What alternative packages could be designed to celebrate a festival?

(e) Can you design and construct a machine which puts an exact amount of sweets into each tube?

(f) If you picked 10 Smarties at random, what colour combinations might you have?

While working on these open-ended tasks the children will need to plan their actions, utilize appropriate mechanical skills and present their findings in an effective and lucid manner to an audience. Each project will involve using many aspects of applicable mathematics and could be completed from a variety of skill levels. Children will be encouraged to utilize cross-curricular skills and a variety of modern presentation techniques, visual aids, desk-top publishing and IT. Projects would provide essential experiences from a wide mathematical base and therefore adequately satisfy the statutory content, particularly AT1 and AT9, 'Using and applying mathematics'. Such an approach not only delivers the requirements of the National Curriculum but also encourages and develops child autonomy. Though the starting points are teacher defined it is important the mathematics becomes owned by the children as soon as possible. They should have total responsibility from initial planning to final presentation. As previously suggested, it will be necessary to compare the planned activities with the prescribed content of the ATs not only as an ongoing record of children's experience but also as a reminder to teachers of mathematical experiences which might have been overlooked. A completed scope chart for this topic clearly highlights aspects of prescribed content covered and elements which require attention at a later date.

| Question, tasks | Attainment targets | Support level |
|---|---|---|
| A, B, C, D, E, F | AT1 Using and applying ATs 1–8 | 1, 2, 3, 4, 5 |
| A, B, C, D, E, F | AT2 Number and number notation | 1, 2, 3, 4 |
| A, B, C, D, E, F | AT3 Number operations | 1, 2, 3, 4 |
| A, B, C, D, E, F | AT4 Estimate and approximate number | 1, 2, 3, 4, 5 |
| A, C, F | AT5 Patterns, relationships and sequences | 1, 2, 3, 4 |
| A, B | AT6 Functions, formulae, equations and inequalities | 2, 3, 4 |
| | AT7 Graphical representation of algebraic functions | |
| B, D, E | AT8 Appreciate nature of measurement | 1, 2, 3, 4, 5 |
| A, B, C, D, E, F | AT9 Shape and space and handle data in practical tasks | 1, 2, 3, 4, 5, 6 |
| B, D, E | AT10 Shape and space—2D and 3D | 1, 2, 3, 4, 5, 6 |
| B, D, E | AT11 Location and transformation in the study of space | 1, 2, 3, 4 |
| A, B, C, F | AT12 Collect, record and process data | 1, 2, 3, 4, 5, 6 |
| A, B, C, F | AT13 Represent and interpret data | 1, 2, 3, 4, 5 |
| A, C, F | AT14 Understand, estimate and calculate probabilities | 1, 2, 3, 4 |

Topic: Mathematical Smarties          Age: Top Junior

As so much emphasis has been placed upon the legal requirement to teach discrete ATs, to tackle planning in this manner
might appear subversive, but it is a strategy which supports
current good practice, initiates an open learning environment
yet still satisfies the legal requirement to supply information for
assessment profiles at key reporting stages. This approach is
endorsed by both the mathematics NSG and the NCC paper,
*A Framework for the Primary Curriculum* (NCC, 1989b). The
alternative, to design programmes of study for a mixed ability
class which target discrete mathematical skills at specific levels,
must have a detrimental effect upon children who do not fit into
the age-related norm. Open-ended mathematical tasks allow the
children freedom to demonstrate their full potential and provide
teachers with the information necessary to record their capabilities and achievements adequately.

It is essential that teachers offer children the opportunity to
work outside the prescribed limits and defined areas. The
National Curriculum is not carved in stone, but is open to modification both through pupil achievement and changes in curriculum content. Curriculum content should also be continually
evaluated to support and reflect technological and social changes.
This is particularly true in the area of information technology,
which will soon form an important part of a pupil's entitlement.

Throughout this chapter mathematics has been addressed as a
discrete element of the primary curriculum. However, learning,
particularly in primary schools, has always been through multidisciplinary experiences. No lesson is exclusively subject specific;
links are made between all curriculum areas to strengthen individual skills and to build a secure framework of life skills. Teachers should continue to offer children multidisciplinary experiences through thematic topic work. To restate an earlier
comment, skills (ATs) are a resource and as such need to be in
a usable form; for the craft of mathematics to be of any value,
children must be given the opportunity and the freedom to utilize
skills within realistic contexts. It is unfortunate that the NSG has
omitted to emphasize other aspects of mathematics which would
add personality to an otherwise utilitarian function. Imaginative
teachers should continue to develop mathematics through a variety of cross-curricular topics: mathematics through aspects of
art, festivals, or the environment. Though the National Curricu-

lum dismembers the curriculum into discrete subject areas for the purpose of assessment and record-keeping it is the task before teachers to reassemble the jigsaw.

## REFERENCES

Burton, L. (1986) *Girls into Maths Can Go.* London: Cassell.

Centre for Mathematics Education, Open University (1986) *Girls into Mathematics.* Milton Keynes: Open University in association with ILEA.

DES (1985) *Curriculum Matters: Mathematics from 5 to 16.* London: HMSO.

DES (1989a) *Curriculum Matters: Information Technology from 5 to 16.* London: HMSO.

DES (1989b) *Report on Information Technology in Initial Teacher Training.* London: HMSO.

DES and Welsh Office (1982) *Mathematics Counts. Report of the Committee of Inquiry into the Teaching of Mathematics.* London: HMSO.

DES and Welsh Office (1990) *Technology in the National Curriculum.* London: HMSO.

NCC (1989a) *Mathematics: Non-statutory Guidance.* York: NCC.

NCC (1989b) *Curriculum Guidance 1: A Framework for the Primary Curriculum.* York: NCC.

# Chapter 8

# Implementing the National Curriculum for Science

*Ron Ritchie*

This chapter explores the issues involved in the practical implementation of the National Curriculum for science. It begins with an examination of the major changes that will be required by the National Curriculum and then identifies what this will mean for class teachers, for science co-ordinators in schools and for headteachers. The second part of the chapter includes two detailed case studies which describe the preparations made for implementing the National Curriculum in an infant school and a junior school. In the first school the staff have only recently begun to develop the science curriculum and their experiences are typical of many schools. The teachers in the second school have been addressing the problem for a longer period. Both schools are exploring creative responses to the National Curriculum that allow the teachers to continue to work in the way they consider most appropriate for their children. The chapter concludes with comments on the case studies, drawing out common threads and attempting to isolate factors which lead to success.

## MAJOR CHANGES REQUIRED BY THE NATIONAL CURRICULUM FOR SCIENCE

It was noted in Chapter 1 that there is a good deal of evidence to show that science has received little systematic attention in many primary schools. Of the three core subjects in the National Curriculum, then, it is science which will necessitate the most significant changes to practice in the majority of primary schools. These changes will involve more than minor adjustments to the classroom curriculum and will have far-reaching consequences for school and classroom management. The changes are listed here and briefly discussed.

## Finding time for science

There is little doubt that the majority of primary teachers will need to spend more time on science. Although the orders do not specify a particular time allocation, there seems to be an expectation that at least an eighth of available school time should be devoted to science. The difficulties of providing evidence of this time being spent is highly problematic. This is particularly true if the integrated approach, favoured by most primary teachers, is adopted. It seems likely that teachers will have to demonstrate how their planning allows for the appropriate time to be devoted to science and the other core curriculum areas.

## Planning science

The requirement to plan work within a defined framework will be new to some primary teachers. Although many primary schools have developed school science policies few have defined the skills, knowledge and understanding that should be taught in the way that the National Curriculum requires. Most teachers have been able to plan their own schemes of work in isolation and to respond to the particular interests, circumstances and enthusiasm of their children. Whole-school curriculum planning will now be vital to ensure continuity. This will have the positive benefits of encouraging teachers to plan and work collaboratively.

Perhaps, however, the biggest demand on teachers will concern the implementation of science within an integrated curriculum. The structure of the National Curriculum and the differences between the approach adopted in the core areas add to this difficulty. Most teachers have, in the past, identified aspects of science that link with their chosen topic. This will now need to be done in a far more systematic way and working on topics with a science focus will necessarily be more frequent. The important links between science and design and technology will require particular attention.

In terms of planning schemes of work there is an inherent danger that some teachers will adopt a curriculum led by attainment targets (ATs). One way of avoiding this is to use, as the non-statutory guidance (NSG) suggests, the programmes of study when planning schemes of work and not the ATs (NCC, 1989, p. A9). A simple, but practical, start can be made by moving the pages in the National Curriculum files that list the programmes of study from the back of the file to the front! Schools may also find it useful to produce their own version of the National Curriculum with the relevant programme of study displayed alongside each AT as they were presented in the Science Working Group's report (DES and Welsh Office, 1988).

It will be necessary for teachers to ensure the progressive development of skills and knowledge and understanding in children. It is here that the explicit levels of attainment with each AT will provide teachers with clear guidance about the nature of progression.

## Developing knowledge and understanding alongside skills

The fact that the National Curriculum defines knowledge and understanding in detail will impose considerable demands on teachers who lack some of the background knowledge themselves. Teachers will now need to adopt an approach to science teaching that recognizes the relationship between the two profile components, 'Exploration of science' and 'Knowledge and understanding'. In the words of the Science Working Group, 'For the child learning science, as for the scientist, the way understanding is developed depends both on the existing ideas and on the process by which those ideas are used and tested in new situations' (DES and Welsh Office, 1988, p. 7).

Providing an investigative approach to science and avoiding a crude attempt to teach the facts must remain a high priority for schools. This is helped by the wording used in the National Curriculum. The programmes of study constantly invite investigation — 'They should investigate the forces involved in floating and sinking' (key stage 2) (DES and Welsh Office, 1989, p. 70) — and the definition of statements of attainment are such that they cannot be taught by rote learning: 'Be able to relate knowledge of these properties to the everyday uses of these materials' (AT 6; DES and Welsh Office, 1989, p. 14).

## Assessing children

Few teachers have consciously assessed children's scientific development in the past and so new skills will be required to carry out teacher assessments and to administer standard assessment tasks (SATs). Linked to this is the need to keep appropriate records, which will have to cover the experiences offered to the children as well as the progress individuals make as a result of those experiences. Peter Ovens outlined the task facing teachers in a *Primary Science Review* editorial:

> Teachers need the flexibility to teach for investigative science, and assess it with open-mindedness to the richness and diversity of responses. To advance the professional quality of our assessment, we need to develop our ability to gather more descriptive information within routine teaching as well as within particular assessment-oriented tasks, about how and what children learn. Most of all, we need to reduce the subjectivity of our assessments by exchanging these descriptions with each other, in discussion about what we learn when we help each other to stand back from our teaching experience. (Ovens, 1989, p. 9)

## Providing the necessary resources

The implementation of the National Curriculum for science will have resource implications in some schools, although these are unlikely to be as serious as might be anticipated. There is undoubtedly a need for certain specialist equipment, such as electrical items and newtonmeters, that some schools will have to purchase. However, schools that have already looked at the resources needed have found that much of the work can be carried out using everyday items which are already in school or which can easily be collected. Perhaps a more important issue to be tackled in this respect is the storage and organization of resources and equipment so that they get used.

## Making the most of information technology

Few primary teachers have exploited information technology in their science work and the explicit reference to the use of computers in AT12 (DES and Welsh Office, 1989, p. 26) and various other programmes of study will require teachers to explore this. There are a number of applications where the computer can be used as a valuable tool to support science (MAPE, 1989). The use of databases to store, and allow the interrogation of, information collected during an investigation is an obvious area. However, the use of word processors to facilitate the collaborative write-up of an investigation planned and carried out by a group can allow the computer to enhance practical work. Data-logging, which allows the computer to take in information directly from an investigation and display it, is another application of considerable potential.

## Equal opportunities and equal access

The National Curriculum is intended to provide a minimum entitlement for all children. If this is to be turned into a reality there are a number of issues to which schools will have to pay particular attention. Children with special educational needs should have, whenever possible, access to the full science curriculum. Little support material is available for teachers in this area but it is one that the NCC has promised to address in later non-statutory information.

Gender issues need addressing if girls are to be provided with genuine equal opportunities. The importance of social contexts for motivating girls in science and the problems sometimes produced by classroom organization and grouping are all well documented and schools need to produce appropriate guidelines to deal with their particular needs and circumstances. In a similar way, the needs of pupils from ethnic minority groups, especially those with English as a second language, should be identified and met. Schools should avoid an ethnocentric model of science in which the achievements of other cultures are ignored, and adopt a multicultural approach which can enrich and enhance the curriculum of every school.

## WHAT DO THESE CHANGES MEAN FOR THE CLASS TEACHER?

In order to bring about these changes most teachers will need to develop knowledge, understanding, skills and attitudes in both the *scientific* and the *professional* dimensions.

### Scientific knowledge and understanding

HMI and others have indicated that teachers will need knowledge of science that is at some level above that expected of the children they teach. This is reflected in DES funding (announced in July 1989) for science courses for primary teachers which are planned to develop their knowledge of science as well as their skills for implementation in the classroom. Alongside this knowledge teachers need an enthusiasm for, and awareness of, the processes involved in science.

### Professional knowledge and skills

In addition to their knowledge and understanding of scientific ideas and concepts, teachers also need to understand the nature of children's learning in science, the way learning in science relates to their general learning and the part which children's language and communication play in their knowledge and understanding in science.

Teachers will need to be able to plan coherently a scheme of work within a school policy for science and then to organize the necessary practical activities in the classroom. Such work requires particular skills in the evaluation and selection of appropriate curriculum materials and the safe and effective organization of such equipment and materials, including information technology, in the classroom.

Teaching and learning in science has implications for classroom interaction: the teacher's use of questions which provoke scientific thinking and her response to individual children's questions are particularly important teaching and learning strategies in science. Teachers therefore need to develop strategies for responding to individual children's initiatives and needs. In making decisions about both planning and classroom interaction teachers must be able to counter gender and ethnic bias: they need to be aware of the latent dangers in, for example, responding excessively to the initiatives of boys.

Assessment and record-keeping are important aspects of the National Curriculum and teachers need to be able to evaluate ongoing classroom work in science, to assess children as an integral part of such work, keep records of individual children's progress and, finally, to administer and score SATs.

## THE ROLE OF THE SCIENCE CO-ORDINATOR

The teacher with curriculum responsibility for science in the school has a crucial role to play in the major developments which need to be made in most schools. The support the science co-ordinator needs to give includes that set out here.

The co-ordinator's central role is to facilitate the writing and review of school policies for science and the development of whole-school schemes of work. This will also involve supporting colleagues in planning and implementing work in the classroom and helping with the selection, purchase, storage and maintenance of equipment and materials, including out-of-school resources such as environmental areas. Working collaboratively with teachers in their classrooms is also very desirable. This support should be formalized by identifying staff development needs in science, recommending external courses and providing school-based in-service days for science workshops and discussions.

Specific skills in assisting those children with special needs, including high achievers, are necessary and these need to be developed in collaboration with colleagues.

The co-ordinator's role extends beyond the school to liaison with governors and parents in order to communicate the aims of the school's science programme and to provide a context in which the children's progress is reported. Parents as well as other adults are often able to assist with science activities in the classroom and the organization of this resource can be profitably managed by the co-ordinator. Liaison is also necessary with other schools, in particular any feeder schools – infant schools, nurseries and playgroups – and the secondary schools to which the children will later move.

Finally, the co-ordinator needs to keep herself and colleagues up to date with local and national initiatives. Liaison with outside agencies, such as the Association for Science Education, is important here.

## THE ROLE OF THE HEADTEACHER

During this time of dramatic development in school science the role of the headteacher is most significant in supporting and encouraging the teachers. The headteacher needs to be committed to science and to making that commitment evident to teachers and pupils.

The science co-ordinator's role needs to be clearly defined and made explicit to other staff. The co-ordinator's work should be further supported by the allocation of in-service days and meetings for staff development, encouraging staff to attend appropriate in-service courses and by encouraging collaboration between members of staff and the co-ordinator. The headteacher should ensure that staff are working to the school schemes and that guidelines have been developed. In doing this there is the responsibility to ensure that adequate funds are available for science resources and that the resources are readily available to teachers through, if necessary, provision of adequate storage facilities.

The headteacher's general monitoring roles include evaluating the teaching of science in the school and making good any deficiencies, ensuring that appropriate records are maintained by staff of science work covered and the progress of individuals and that staff have access to necessary records. Finally, the head-teacher should be involved in liaison at the LEA level, ensuring that LEA guidelines are followed, where appropriate.


## SCIENCE IN ACTION – TWO CASE STUDIES

This chapter has so far shown what developments are necessary at the different levels in the school. In this section it will explore the ways in which an infant school and a junior school have attempted to meet the challenge of the new developments required by the National Curriculum.


### Case study 1 – Moorlands Infant School, Bath

Moorlands Infant School occupies a 1950s building on the edge of a large council estate on the southern side of Bath. There are eight classes and all the teachers are enthusiastic, open-minded and committed. There is always evidence around the school of practical activities being carried out with the children, but some staff express a lack of confidence in science. Preparations for implementing the National Curriculum in science at Moorlands began in earnest in July 1988. When Liz Thomas was interviewed for a new job at the school she was asked if she would be prepared to accept responsibility for science. Although this was not an area she regarded as one of her strengths she was happy to agree, as science had always been one of her interests.

Liz Thomas describes the first year in her new role and shows how she was able to help her colleagues to develop their work in science.

*Soon after beginning my new job in September 1988, I enrolled on a primary science and technology course at a local college. I was somewhat unsure of what it might involve but soon found myself constructing models, testing wallpapers and wiring up circuits. All the staff at the school were really interested to hear about the course and my attempts to try out activities with my class of middle infants. We soon developed the custom of discussing each week's sessions informally in the staffroom and staff would drop into the classroom to see work in progress. This was important to me and, I hope, to the other staff concerned.*

*The head was very supportive of my approach and during that term she asked me to present displays of science work for children and other staff to see. My first display was of a skeleton and included a number of X-rays. This linked in with my own class topic on hospitals. It was interesting to look at but did not involve as much active participation as I would have liked.*

*Just before half-term, I decided to attend a 'Primary Science Night' at a local teachers' centre. These are informal occasions organized by advisory teachers and open to all teachers. It was a chance to talk to other teachers interested in science and I saw a fascinating display of 'fastenings' (string, tapes, zips, clasps), together with suggested activities. This provided the second of the term's displays in school! I tried hard to make the display 'active' and my class did some valuable sorting and classifying work from it. The most relevant aspect that developed from this work was our contribution to the Christmas entertainment. We did a sketch about Father Christmas wrapping presents with different materials and different fastenings. This had the advantage of everyone in the school becoming aware of our work — there is a tendency for displays to get missed! My class also invented a game that involved guessing the criteria used to produce particular sortings. This game was taken around to other classes by my children and this encouraged further discussion about science activities.*

*During the spring term science become more prominent in school and more staff were including it in their classroom work. I think this was partly because I was finding the science that I was including in my work so interesting and this was rubbing off on other staff. I talked about it a great deal and other members of staff showed genuine interest and began to reciprocate and share their own classroom experiences. Soon, there seemed to be an almost endless stream of children going around the school 'sharing' their science activities with other classes. We regularly included a number of our most interesting science investigations in our weekly 'sharing assembly' and this again stimulated staff interest and led to some of the activities being replicated in other classes. Well over half the staff were now telling me about their science work and I passed on their successes to other teachers even if they, themselves, were too reticent to do so.*

*At this time we received a copy of the Avon LEA new* Primary Science Guidelines *(Avon, 1989). This was being produced by the primary science advisory teachers in response to the National Curriculum. I read it several times and although I found it enormously helpful in most respects, it posed one terrible problem for us. It suggested a way of delivering the National Curriculum which involved a whole staff adopting particular topics for each half term (Avon, 1989, p. 22). These were specified for the whole school and neither I, nor anyone on our staff, wanted to be told what topic to follow each term. We all felt very strongly that to deprive us of our freedom to choose our topics would reduce our interest in, and commitment to, our topic work. The problem was made worse by two other factors. Firstly, we did not wish the reception class teachers to be under any obligation to cover large areas of the science curriculum as we felt that very young children, and often their teachers, were under enough pressure already. Secondly, we have two classes of mixed age groups, which in any case made the suggested grid of negotiated topics unworkable.*

*While we were tussling with this seemingly insoluble problem, we had a staff in-service day. We had agreed to free part of this day to discuss the up-to-date information that the three core curriculum subject co-ordinators had available. This gave us an opportunity to get together as a staff and identify what we felt were the common links throughout the National Curriculum that would support our attempts to provide a child-centred education. In my contribution I stressed the importance of the first profile component, 'Exploration of science', and this helped clarify the importance of the way children work in science and countered the view that the National Curriculum was just a set of facts to teach.*

*We followed this day with a number of staff meetings at which we discussed how we could cover profile component 2 ('knowledge and understanding') without constructing a rigid syllabus or using the LEA's grid approach. We tried dividing the content areas into sections for different classes, but this proved difficult to do and the result was unsatisfactory. I then realized suddenly that we could organize it in a completely different way by grouping those ATs which could be taught through an ongoing approach and those that lent themselves to a specific topic. The latter group was then divided into two further groups which seemed to be reasonably balanced. This meant that in any one school year all our*

*classes containing either middle or top infants would agree to cover the ongoing ATs and one of the other groups. The following year, the ongoing targets would continue to be covered along with the group not tackled in the previous year.*
*The following groups were involved:*

*Attainment targets to be covered by ongoing work*

| | | | |
|---|---|---|---|
| AT1 | Exploration of science | AT9 | Earth and atmosphere |
| AT2 | Variety of life | | (observing the weather) |
| AT4 | Genetics and evolution | AT12 | Information technology |
| AT5 | Human influences on the Earth | AT16 | The earth in space |

| *Group A – Topic Approach* | *Group B — Topic Approach* |
|---|---|
| AT3 Processes of life | AT6 Types and uses of |
| AT9 Earth and atmosphere | materials |
| AT10 Forces | AT11 Electricity |
| AT15 Light | AT13 Energy |
| | AT14 Sounds and music |

*Everyone seemed pleased with this way of covering the National Curriculum and at the same time retaining our freedom to choose our own topics. We have decided to try this for a year and then review the situation the following summer.*

*We realized that covering the National Curriculum in this way will put quite a strain on our limited resources. Inevitably, we all began discussing the organization of resources. At that time most of our science resources were stored in a central cupboard. Because of the geography of the school we decided to set up two more areas in each of our corridors. This will mean that all classes are close enough for children to able to help themselves to equipment. Certain items, like magnifiers, sellotape, paper, card, fasteners, scissors, staplers and measuring equipment were to be stored on open shelves in each classroom. The other units would contain items which we wished to have readily available but which we could not afford to have in each classroom. These included saws, jigs, wood, dowel, wheels, springs, magnets and electrical equipment. The central store would contain equipment that was in short supply and not in regular use like prisms, glue gun, compasses and our collections.*

*Another priority is to extend the number of 'collections' we have available for classroom use. We all find these a practical way of developing science in the classroom and have decided to put together a central resource of 'collections'. This will include collections of shells, rocks, bones, fabrics, woods, papers, markers, gloves, bottles, shiny things, metal things, strings and threads, stretchy things etc. They will all be supported by sheets of possible activities and other resource material as appropriate. Each member of staff will have a list of our collections and other equipment and resources, such as TV programmes, that we have available in school. I have established a science resource shelf in the staff-room where I put the published schemes and other materials that we have purchased or collected. They used to be kept in the science cupboard but I feel they are more readily available and, therefore, more likely to be used if kept in a prominent and convenient place.*

*At the beginning of the summer term (1989) we had an in-service day that concentrated on science and the National Curriculum. This was planned and organized in consultation with the staff by two of the LEA's advisory teachers for science. The day was essentially practical and proved an invaluable opportunity for exploration and discussion. It certainly kept up the momentum for change and it was natural that, following this day, we would start discussions about our school science policy.*

*The formulation of a science policy dominated our regular weekly staff meetings for the first half of term. It was agreed that our policy should be a statement about the philosophy which underpins our science teaching. By half-term the first draft had been written and included the following:*

*Science for young children means exploring, discovering and investigating the world around them. This means that all children entering our infant school bring some experience of science with them. We hope to start by listening to the children in our care so that we know what ideas they already have about how and why things happen. If we listen to them, we will be in a better position to give them experiences which will help them to clarify their ideas. In essence this means that our science teaching will be child-centred. . . .*

*In our culture scientific knowledge and understanding are changing all the time, but if our children are taught to use scientific skills these will always be needed. So the methods which the children use to learn are at least as important as the facts they learn. Science is the search for, rather than the answer to, questions of why and how. . . .*

*We will try to choose scientific activities which stimulate the natural curiosity of the children. . . .*

*We hope to foster a positive attitude towards science by ensuring that the children enjoy scientific activities and that they find them useful. They should be encouraged to express their ideas in their own terms and use their new found knowledge about how things happen in their everyday lives in school. . . .*

*We will take positive steps to ensure that any child who may have a poor self-image in relation to science activities is given the opportunity to work in a sheltered and nurturing environment.*

*The policy also included a set of aims outlining what we hoped to achieve in terms of developing science. We are also drawing up schemes of work which contain guidance on how to put the policy into action in the classroom. These include help on identifying multicultural aspects of science work, on providing equal opportunities for all children and supporting those children with special educational needs. We have several children in a hearing-impaired unit and their needs require attention.*

*Throughout this term, we tried to identify in our forecasts of work the programmes of study and ATs that we will be working on in mathematics and science. We saw this as a trial run for the full implementation of the National Curriculum in September 1989.*

*The sharing of the children's science work at assemblies and through visits to other classes continued and became an established part of school life. We also tried hard to give the children opportunities to show their parents their science work as we recognized that this was important to help to communicate to parents what we were trying to achieve in our science work. We have always encouraged the involvement of parents in the classroom and naturally this has often meant their working on science-related activities. The next phase of our development of science is to include a hands-on science evening for parents.*

*Our discussions during the year have also addressed another of our major anxieties, which concerned record-keeping. We are considering having three record sheets for each child in their record folder: one for ongoing ATs and one each for the other two groups listed earlier. These will not be tick sheets but will be used to note relevant activities the child has experienced and any evidence of significant achievements made by the child. We plan to review this approach at a later in-service day when we examine the problem of record-keeping right across the curriculum. This will also include an opportunity for us to explore the ways in which we are assessing individual children's progress.*

*Linked to our development of science has been a growing awareness of the need to provide more technological experiences for our children, particularly through a more effective use of the constructional equipment we have in school. When children put their scientific knowledge to some practical use, by designing and making something themselves, is takes on a real purpose for them. In this context we realize it is important to give them the right sort of challenge. Design and technology is, however, a new area for almost all of us; but we are making a beginning. One class set about designing kites recently as part of their topic on China, another class were making bags as an aspect of their topic on shopping. Our developments in this area have been supported by an in-service morning at a local college on 'designing and making' activities.*

*I am pleased that another member of staff has expressed an interest in going on the in-service course that I recently finished. I feel that I would like to go on a second-level course in a year's time. In particular, a course that helps me a little more with my own background knowledge of science would be useful. The next year will be devoted to putting into practice what I have learnt so far and helping others to do the same. As a staff we are enthusiastic about our science teaching but we are all very aware that we have only just made a start in developing effective science teaching that will provide all of our children with a rich and relevant science curriculum to prepare them for life in the twenty-first century.*

## Case study 2 – Summerhill Junior School, Bristol

Summerhill is a junior school on the edge of Bristol's inner city. There are nine classes in this old Victorian building, which has recently benefited from a new extension and refurbishment. The head has been in post four years and has had the opportunity to appoint several new staff, including four probationers. The present staff are firm believers in the philosophy of child-centred, integrated and independent learning. They are all committed to the teaching of science and technology and have chosen to adopt a problem-solving approach, reflecting their belief that children learn best through tackling open-ended challenges.

Recently, the National Curriculum has heightened every primary teacher's awareness of the importance of science. But at Summerhill, under the influence of its head, they have been developing their science curriculum for a number of years.

The head, Kate St John, describes her commitment to science in these terms,

> As someone who cut her 'teaching teeth' over twenty years ago on forty-five family-grouped infants in a hut in the playground I found that the only way to establish order, retain my sanity and excite creativity, interest and enthusiasm in my class was to indulge in 'science'. It worked and I became even more addicted to questioning, reasoning, probing, thinking around corners and the like and have remained so ever since.

Her first, and most significant, step was to enlist the help of the LEA advisory team for science and technology for about eighteen months, from January 1986 to July 1987. The first phase of this support involved a foray into 'fast thinker' activities. This provided a structured and manageable experience for teachers, whilst *opening new and exciting doors for children.* Children began working together in *a controlled yet liberated way, finding out about structures and forces, materials and energy — not to mention relationships — as they constructed towers out of straws, marble-run timers and packages for Easter eggs!* Initially these activities were organized in isolation from other classroom activities and it took some time before a few staff found the confidence and commitment to employ the approach as an integral part of their classroom repertoire. Much emphasis was placed on the problem-solving approach to learning, but it did seem as if, for most of the period, the words *fell on stony ground.*

It became clear that what was needed to really make the difference throughout the school was an enthusiastic and determined science co-ordinator. Such a person was appointed as the curriculum leader for science and technology in September 1987 and the school has not looked back since.

The curriculum leader, Hayley Smith, takes up the story:

On my appointment, I soon realized that I had joined a team of enthusiastic and co-operative colleagues, all of whom were teaching science to some degree. What was needed was a structured and more uniform approach that allowed for continuity and progression. It was clear that there was a need for staff development activities which reassured everyone that they were in fact teaching science, even if they weren't labelling it as such.

Through a series of weekly after-school meetings we established what we wanted for our school science policy. This started from identifying our strengths and weaknesses. These sessions also included a variety of 'hands on' activities to widen our experiences of investigations that encouraged the development of scientific skills, concepts and attitudes as outlined in the LEA's science guidelines.

In September 1988, we used one of our allocated in-service training days for science. The morning involved practical workshops for the staff and the afternoon found us brainstorming topic webs and examining the programmes of study from the National Curriculum science report (DES and Welsh Office, 1988). During this term, we used our nine-tenths part-time teacher to release me to work alongside other teachers developing their science work. This meant each class had two teachers for a whole day each fortnight to work on science activities. This had a significant effect on the children and one teacher expressed a view shared by many at the time, 'I can actually see the changes in some children — they're co-operating more and showing enthusiasm for what they do.' At the end of term, we held our annual Christmas problem-solving day. Parents, students and other friends of the school are invited in to help the children solve problems, set by the staff, on a Christmas theme. Many parents commented positively on the attitudes and abilities demonstrated by the children as they tackled this work. A parents' workshop on science capitalized on this enthusiasm and laid the foundations for a genuine home–school partnership.

One of the most important developments from the INSET received by the staff at this time was a more thorough and confident approach to their planning of science and technology. It was evident that they had vastly improved their knowledge of scientific skills; their topic webs included activities to develop observation, sorting and classifying and testing etc. They were also identifying *opportunities, often through the use of collections, for children to formulate and test their own hypotheses.*

*Figure 8.1 illustrates how a topic, for third- and fourth-year juniors, on 'Flight' was planned and the science opportunities that were identified.*

*However, at this time little thought was given to continuity and progression and there was virtually no reference to the content of our science programme. We were much more concerned with the processes involved. At the planning level, there needed to be more clarification of the concepts being developed by the activities identified. At this point we also began to look more closely at the programmes of study and ATs and these provided added reason for addressing content, as well as process, in our school guidelines and in our classroom work. Teachers continued to produce their webs but now included reference to particular programmes of study and ATs as Figure 8.2, 'Life Aspects', illustrates.*

*At Summerhill, therefore, there was a warm reception for the National Curriculum for science. The framework provided fitted well with the policy the school was developing. Our next task was to become more familiar with its requirements. After much deliberation, we eventually decided to answer its requirements of 'Pupils should . . .' with a scheme of work which included, 'Teachers could . . .'.*

*Working in pairs, all the staff took a particular AT, examined it carefully, and created a resource bank of ideas and activities that could be used to provide appropriate experiences for children. In the school policy document itself I was careful to state that 'What follows is a detailed scheme of work for science which, we feel, will satisfy the requirements of the National Curriculum', and to stress:*

> *It is important to note (here) that this document is not an exhaustive list. The Summerhill guidelines suggest that, 'Teachers could . . .', not that, 'Teachers should . . .'. You and the pupils you teach may have other ideas!*

*This is an example taken from the scheme of work which covers AT15, 'Using light.'*

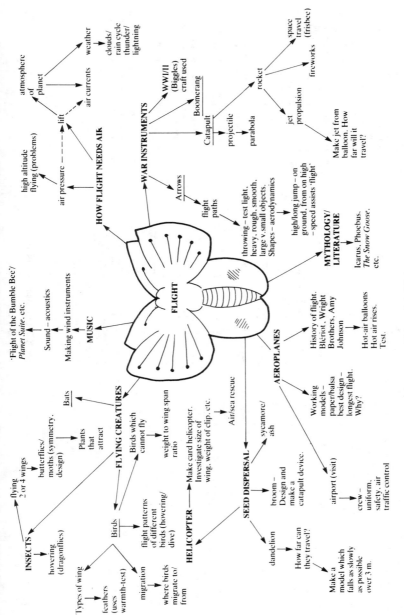

**Figure 8.1** Flight

## SCIENCE AND TECHNOLOGY (AT10)

*Level 2*: House demolished by war. Ways of moving debris. Use spring balance to measure force needed to move brick by dragging, lifting, sledging, runners, rollers, wheels. Which is easiest way to move load?

*Level 3*: Travelling along a bumpy road. Which surface would be hardest for a lorry to move over? Design fair test using toy car.

Parachutes: Demonstrate drag by flapping card through air. What is difference in movement of flat piece of A4 paper and screwed-up A4 falling through the air?
Make parachute. Real parachutes have a hole in the top. Test the difference that this makes.
– Change material used.
– Does shape make any difference?

Boats: A boat is blown up. Predict which of a group of objects would sink or float. Test.

*Level 4*: Use slopes of varying inclines. What force is needed to stop a toy car?

Rubber band tanks/ wind-driven machines. What happens with greater no. of turns of matchstick/ increased rate of air?

(AT11) Design a model tank or lorry. Put two headlights on the front of it.

(AT1) Level 5/6 Make 3 parachutes of diff. sizes. Two loads of diff. masses to be carried slowly to ground. Which parachute would be best for each load?

## MATHS

(AT3 L3, AT8 L3, 4, AT10 L2, 4, AT12 L3)
– measurement of time using different measures
– digital & analogue clocks
– recognition of shapes
– measurement of angles (acute/obtuse/reflex)
– sorting shapes
– construction of 2D/ 3D shapes

## LANGUAGE

*Speaking & listening (L3)*
Drama – how children would feel if evacuated
(L3) learn poem from 1940s.
(L4) report on problem-solving exercises.
(L5) to volunteer for war or not?
Discuss pros and cons.
*Writing* (AT1, AT2)
(L3, L4) write about a day in 1940.
Revise, redraft
*Reading* (AT1, AT2)
(L3) comprehension on topic
(L4) discuss poems / research topic

**LIFE ASPECTS**

**1940s**

## GEOGRAPHY

Comparison of 1940s maps with up-to-date ones.

Building styles

questionnaires

Where did war take place?

Evacuation
– Where? Why?

Make dramatic reconstructions.

## HISTORY

Use of primary & secondary sources to research various aspects of life during 1940s.
e.g. evacuation
school
women
blitz
rations
shelters etc.

## RE

Aspects of Jewish life
cf. Christianity
(PSE) peace/conflict/ violence.

## ART

– Use of pen & ink/ pastels to draw wartime artefacts
– Enlarge 1940s posters (paint)
– Frieze of WWII street scene

## MUSIC

– 1940s songs
– composing music to give sense of happiness/ sadness

## TECHNOLOGY

– Make a bridge to span a gap of 2 m.
– Look at WWII machinery. Make models using construction apparatus.
– Design a model of a Morrison shelter. Make using wood technique.

**Figure 8.2** Life aspects: 1940s

## Attainment target 15 — Light

| Pupils should . . . | Teachers could . . . |
| --- | --- |
| — know that light can be made to change direction and that shiny surfaces form images | 1. Ask the children to collect shiny things, e.g. spoons, mirrors, metal objects, tinfoil, etc. Sort and investigate the collection according to how well the objects reflect. |
| — be able to give an account of an investigation with mirrors | 2. Ask the children to draw their reflection. Can they see their friends in the mirrors? Can they make multiple images? What happens if you use a curved mirror? 3. Ask them to use mirrors to see around corners. 4. Challenge them to make periscopes and kaleidoscopes. |

Putting together these ideas took quite a long time but it proved to be a valuable exercise for all concerned and helped us become familiar with the detail of the National Curriculum.

Although we see the National Curriculum as a framework for our science we are very clear that it is a minimum requirement. Listening to and observing children may lead to activities and discussions, based on their existing ideas, that are not included in the programmes of study or our schemes of work. We are also clear that the National Curriculum need not challenge our philosophy of education; we will not be teaching science as a timetabled isolated subject but will continue to view it as an integrated part of the whole curriculum. This has been evident in all our collaborative planning sessions and discussions. However, a very positive result of the National Curriculum has been a more careful and thorough approach to planning work for children that refers to skills and concepts and allows for continuity and progression. There are also provisions built in for the underachiever, the average and more able child. Science will be included in the education of all children and hopefully each child can work at their own level and reach their full potential.

*We share some reservations that many schools have about the National Curriculum: whether there will be enough time; how teachers without specialist science skills will manage; how each child will be assessed and whether there will be room for children's and teacher's spontaneity. We are looking for answers to these questions that work for us. Our recent experiences have convinced us that spontaneity need not be lost if teachers are prepared to become familiar with the National Curriculum so that they can capitalize on the child's own questions and ideas and link the unexpected experiences to other ATs that they had not planned to cover.*

*The following is an example of this that began with a present from a child of a bunch of daffodils. This starting point led to a variety of questions and activities. None of these are likely to be new to most teachers, but they were novel experiences for the third-year junior children involved. As a starting point to encourage more careful observation of the flowers a group of children were invited to do pastel drawings of them. This was followed up by getting them to draw more accurate and detailed diagrams, where they researched and labelled the various parts of the flower. 'Why are the daffodils wilting?', asked a child. 'Because they need water', replied another. 'Do they drink water, Miss?', questioned the first child. At this point, of course, like any other primary teacher with a love of science, I said, 'I don't know, how could you find out?'.*

*The examples of work shown in Figure 8.3 illustrate the investigation that followed. The activity offered opportunities for me to assess work related to AT1 ('exploration of science') and AT3 ('process of life'). Perhaps more importantly it was a relevant and motivating activity for the children that integrated science, art, language and information technology.*

## Do daffodils drink water?

We did an experiment to see if daffodils drank water. We got two bottles which we filled with water. Then we put 10 drops of blue food colouring in one bottle and red in the other. We left them for 24 hours.

When this time was up, we cut open the stems. We noticed that the daffodils had absorbed some of the coloured water. The water had risen about a quarter of the way up the stem. We wanted to find out if the water would reach the head.

We set up another test. We left two new daffodils in the same amount of water and food colouring. We left them for one week.

### Conclusions.

After the week was over we found that not only had the stems changed colour, but the heads had changed too. This is what they looked like. This proves that daffodils drink water.

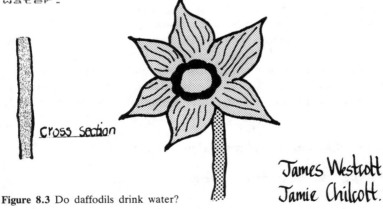

cross section

James Westcott
Jamie Chilcott.

**Figure 8.3** Do daffodils drink water?

*In conclusion, the staff at Summerhill regard the implementation of the National Curriculum for science as an arduous, but not impossible, task. The good primary practice which has been established in the school must continue and we must find a way to make the National Curriculum work with us and not against us!*

## WHAT LEADS TO SUCCESS IN DEVELOPING SCIENCE?

In the examples from the two schools the following common factors seem important in successfully addressing science in the National Curriculum:

### Time

Curriculum change in schools does not occur overnight and to ensure the development of a science curriculum that will deliver the National Curriculum will require schools to commit considerable time and effort. Science had been identified as a priority in both these schools and they had chosen to concentrate on that for a considerable length of time.

### Involvement of the whole staff

A whole-school approach has been achieved in these schools through the active involvement of staff throughout the development. It was significant that teachers in both schools were made aware of the aims of the development. However, change in individual classrooms was constantly under the control of the individual teachers and not imposed from 'above' with the whole school compelled to embrace a sequence of common content or topics. It is important to start from teachers' strengths and from a realistic appraisal of 'where the school is' in terms of science.

### Commitment to a cross-curricular approach

All the teachers involved in these schools were fully committed to an integrated child-centred approach and were determined that the National Curriculum would not cause them to change their strongly held educational philosophy. The adopted a positive, but critical approach to the proposed changes and found their own particular solution to implementation that enriched, rather than impoverished, the education they were providing for the children in their care.

## Supportive headteachers

Without the active support of the headteacher curriculum development is unlikely to prove effective or long-lasting. The heads in the two schools use different management styles but both are totally committed to improving the quality of science teaching going on in their schools. This was demonstrated through support for the co-ordinator and individual teachers both formally, in meetings and interviews, and informally in the staffroom, after assemblies and at parents' evenings. They also provided time for a variety of purposes, ensured resources were provided and available and insisted that staff provide evidence of science in their planning and record-keeping.

## Enthusiastic co-ordinators

The case for a science co-ordinator in schools should no longer need arguing and these schools provide ample evidence of the significant effect an individual can have on curriculum development if they are sensitive to individual staff needs and prepared to 'shout a bit' about what they do. Both of these co-ordinators were proactive and determined to share their successes (and failures) with other staff. They used such strategies as displays, child visits, workshops in the school hall, 'sharing' assemblies, and open classroom doors which encourage other staff to see what's going on and try it for themselves. The opportunity to work alongside colleagues, given to Hayley Smith, can be a particularly productive way of encouraging change. Enabling teachers to see their own children 'doing science' can be a successful way of convincing teachers it will work. School-based workshops, like Summerhill's Christmas problem-solving day, are another way of organizing opportunities for teachers to observe their children engaging in scientific investigations without it being too threatening.

**A school science policy**

The Initiatives in Primary Science and Evaluation (IPSE) project examined factors that influenced change and found that 'The greatest progress has been made in those schools which have evolved a written document slowly, basing it on established classroom practice and though staff discussion' (IPSE, 1988, p. 25).

A policy written at the head's request, by a co-ordinator, simply to satisfy the advisers or inspectors when they visit school is not particularly valuable. However, a policy that develops through whole-staff participation is one that the staff feel they 'own' and one that they are more likely to implement. In both these schools, the process of producing the policy could be argued to be just as important as the final document. The policy is also something that should be constantly under review and reflect the changes in the particular circumstances of the individual schools. Linked to the policy in both these schools is a commitment to a scheme of work. In Moorlands' case, at the present time, this is broadly defined. Summerhill staff are negotiating and writing a more comprehensive one. Both meet the needs of the individual schools. As one teacher said recently, 'There isn't a right answer — we have just got to work out what's best for our school.'

**Opportunities for teachers to engage in science**

The lack of confidence many teachers feel about science is best overcome by providing them with time to try out things for themselves and understand what it means to carry out a scientific investigation. School-based workshops for staff, school in-service days and attendance at LEA and other courses are all ways that these schools used. The need identified by Liz Thomas for courses that address teachers' own background knowledge and understanding in science is an area that LEAs, HMI and other providers of INSET are now tackling. Science is essentially a practical activity and the enthusiasm for science that we hope to engender in children will only become a reality if they are given the opportunity to behave 'scientifically'.

Implementing the National Curriculum for science in primary

schools will be an enormous challenge for many teachers. It provides the opportunity for every child in England and Wales to experience a broad and balanced science curriculum. However, it does not guarantee that science education will be of a high quality. That is the responsibility of individual teachers. Highly committed, enthusiastic and talented teachers have been trying to develop science teaching in primary schools for many years. Although there have been successes, progress has been slow. The Secretary of State, Kenneth Baker, intended to effect significant changes almost overnight. The success of this will depend on teachers understanding the nature of those changes and becoming professionally committed to them. Despite the Secretary of State's intentions it is likely to take a number of years for science to become established in the primary curriculum and good practice to become evident in all our schools. They will be interesting times for us all!

Finally, it is perhaps worth giving the last word to a 6-year-old at Moorlands who reminds us in very simple terms of how important it is to ensure that science builds on children's natural curiosity and is enjoyable and motivating. A group were working with a torch and prism when they discovered they could make a 'rainbow'. There were shrieks of delight and Christopher was overheard to say, 'This might be on the news or in the paper!'

## REFERENCES

Avon LEA (1989) *Primary Science Guidelines*. Bristol: Avon LEA.

DES and Welsh Office (1988) *Science for Ages 5 to 16*. London: DES and Welsh Office.

DES and Welsh Office (1989) *Science in the National Curriculum*. London: HMSO.

IPSE (1988) *School in Focus*. Hatfield: ASE.

Micros and Primary Education (1989) *Primary Science: The Role of Information Technology*. Microscope Special, Birmingham: Newman College.

NCC (1989) *Science: Non-Statutory Guidance*. York: NCC.

Ovens, P. (1989) The National Curriculum and professional assessment. *Primary Science Review* (National Curriculum Special), summer 1989.

Science Working Group (1987) *Interim Report*. London: DES.

# Index